A PLUME BOOK

GONE 'TIL NOVEMBER

LIL WAYNE

PLUME
An imprint of Penguin Random House LLC
375 Hudson Street
New York, New York 10014

IP REGISTERED TRADEMARK—MARCA REGISTRADA
Library of Congress Cataloging-in-Publication Data
has been applied for.

ISBN 978-0-7352-1211-4

Printed in the United States of America
1 3 5 7 9 10 8 6 4 2

Dedicated to Mercedes Carter and Reginald McDonald

Author's Note

Here it is, ladies and gentlemen! The time is right to release *Gone 'Til November* into the world. Because of all the bullshit I'm going through with my record label, I wanted my fans to have something from me while they continue to be ever so amazing and patient. I didn't have plans to publish the journal when I was writing it at Rikers—I was just doing something to pass time in there. It became something to look forward to every night, which is very difficult to do when you're locked up.

This book wasn't written to clear up any misconceptions about my time in prison. If anything, it'll show that I'm a regular motherfucker like everybody else. I was just observing, adjusting in an unusual environment, and trying to find joy in hell.

What I'd like my amazing fans to get out of this whole ordeal is that I love 'em enough to share such personal feelings and experiences. And that you shouldn't ever wanna be in there!!!!!!!!!!!!!!!!!!!!!! I did enough experiencing for you all! Love.

—Wayne

GONE 'TIL NOVEMBER

Still Trying to Believe That It's Real!

For some crazy reason, I keep thinking that I'm going to wake up tomorrow and the judge is gonna say that I don't have to go to jail. I actually showed up to go to jail twice (how crazy is that?) and was told to wait 'til next week. Once just because somebody threatened to burn the courthouse down. So this time, I'm like, Shit, hopefully tomorrow they'll tell me that the court has a bomb in that bitch and I have to come back next week...or even better: Don't worry about it, Mr. Carter, you don't have to report at all. But it didn't happen and I have to go in. Damn!

The reality of "naw, nigga, yo ass is going to jail" is starting to really kick in, so now the primary focus is preparation. Being that I never experienced jail for myself before, I'm just trying to remember all I ever heard from whoever on how to conduct myself up in that bitch. My mind is racing with all of the don't do this, the don't say this, but do say this, the do be like this, and the don't let a nigga do this type of shit that I've ever heard before.

I finally got a grasp on the reality of me going to jail by telling myself to just stay calm, maintain myself, and don't let it get to me too much because I only have to do eight months AND to remember to make sure that this would be the only eight months of my life that I'd ever spend in someone's prison.

I'm hoping like hell to get out of this hell early for good behavior or by my lawyers being able to pull something off.

Isn't it bugged out how only time will tell?

Day 1 up in This Bitch!

I've never been one who doesn't take full responsibility for their actions, but damn, I really don't deserve this. If I hadn't traded my blue Marc Jacobs jeans, white polo, and gray Vans for a green onesie, I wouldn't have believed this shit myself.

In 24 hours, I went from the plush life of having fans ask to take my picture, to the harsh reality of having to take my prisoner ID picture. And just when I thought the moment couldn't get any worse, they snapped the picture while I was talking... damn!

I'm not sure why, but I had to talk to the prison psychiatrist when I got here. I told her that I shouldn't be talking to her because I'm not crazy... but I ended up really enjoying her conversation. Is that crazy? We talked about traveling the world, where we've been and where we would like to go, BUT both of us were in jail... crazy!

Up until this point, everybody that I met was being very helpful. Nobody was being rude. Nobody was being like, Oh nigga, you think you Lil Wayne?! And nobody gave me any extra credit or extra attention either. They all just treated me with respect.

I thought about how COs must see mothafuckas come in this bitch every day and the norm is not to affiliate with them whatsoever. Their mind-set has to be "I'm in here to get a paycheck and YOU'RE in here because you're an inmate, period! We have nothing in common... we can't talk about nothing, nigga!"

But when I walk in, there's an automatic connection because they feel like, oh, I am like this mothafucka though. I know this mothafucka right here. I actually know him. He's not a criminal.

I know he drives a car. I know he has a house. I know he has 2 kids. This being in contrast of thinking, I don't know this mothafucka. This mothafucka will probably steal my purse, or steal out my wallet. Even though I wasn't given any special privileges, I appreciated not being treated like an inmate.

My next conversation didn't go so well. As I was being led to the captain's office, I was still just trying to figure out what I was about to go through. I got lost in the thought of how each step that I made was one step farther from everything that I love. And to what? A world of dysfunction, disrespect, and distrust. Come to think of it, it is sort of like the music biz, only without the female groupies.

So as soon as I sat down in the captain's office, his fucking first words to me were, "Don't fuck with my staff!" Damn! Definitely won't be getting any celebrity treatment from the captain. The whole conversation was him telling me, Don't come in here trying to be what you are. You're not gonna "Lil Wayne" up this mothafucka! You're gonna do this, you're going to do that, AND you're going to shut the fuck up!

So as I sat there quietly...haha...all I was thinking was that since there's nothing else to explain here, I'm done

4

With this dude, so just take me to my cell and I'll stay out of your way. I mean his first exact words were "Don't fuck with my staff." He's probably gonna be an asshole the entire time.

After the captain's great words of discouragement, I was handed a towel, two sheets, a toothbrush, toothpaste, and a green cup. Oh yeah...and a cell...cell 29.

Cell 29 is the last cell before the red gate where they immunize the guys getting tested and shit. I'm guessing it was the warden's orders to assign me cell 29 for whatever reason. I didn't like that as soon as I got there, they were like, "Come on, Aviles, get up...get your shit packed up. This ain't your cell no more. We got to find you another cell...Come on, Aviles." That man was just chilling and they were like pack up and move to another cell, all because here comes Lil Wayne.

I looked at it as since the warden ordered me to be in that mothafucking cell, obviously they already knew I was coming a month ago, so why the fuck would you have somebody in that mothafucka up until the point when I'm standing right outside of it? Was it done just to make a scene?

Wasn't trying to start off on the wrong foot up in this bitch, so I made sure I went up to Aviles later like, Look, my nigga, you know I didn't have anything to do with that shit and I ain't come in this bitch like I want that cell right there. He was like, "Nah, my nigga, I understand, my nigga—they be on some other shit. I ain't tripping." And that was that.

5

I'm glad I cooled that situation down, but the temperature in the cell had to be set on hell. It had to be no less than 99 degrees, all because of a heater that was left on. As soon I heard the cell door lock behind me, I just sat on the back wall and the tears began to flow as I took my first glimpse at my new digs... three buckets, one bed, one toilet that was surprisingly kind of clean (emphasis on "kind of"), a rusty ass sink with a mirror the size of a small notepad, a desk, and a window. A clothesline was left hanging in the cell. I decided to leave it because I figured it would come in handy.

I got in just in time for chow...which is the overall term used for what they call breakfast, lunch, and dinner. I only ate the veggies because I wasn't too sure what the other stuff was. After I was given some juice in my little green cup, an inmate quickly informed me not to drink it. He said if you throw it on the floor, it would stain it. Being that these are some pretty tough floors, I passed on the juice and went with prison faucet water. I'm thinking it should be okay since the water from the sink is ice-cold, and never hot...although brushing my teeth is going to be real interesting, I imagine.

I wasn't in the mood to do much socializing, so I kept the first day meet and greet short. I guess not everybody on staff got the captain's memo, because two COs were suspended for trying to come up and see me...females, of course. Maybe there will be some female groupies in the bitch, after all.

One of the inmates said he met me ten years ago.
I'm thinking, Yeah right! But it turns out that he
actually did.

Fuck...one down!

Welcome 2 Da Family

Woke up at 4am for breakfast "chow." I had coffee that was given to me along with some other "goodies." The guys on my tier made me feel like I was a part of a family they've created amongst themselves...like a brotherhood. I was the new brother and they showed me love just like one. I'll forever be thankful to them for that. They really lightened the harsh blow of reality for me.

All in all, they gave me magazines, tea, some better soap than the prison's soap, an earphone radio, and extra chow.

Didn't ask for none of it, but it goes to show that this place isn't so bad. Well, wait, maybe it is. Maybe this place is so bad. Yeah, it is that bad!

Did a lot of talking today. There's Chris, who gave me the radio. He looks fifteen years old, like he's in here for stealing gum.

There's Avilles, the guy who had to give up his cell for me. He's kind of nervous, but his heart shines through his eyes. He's a good guy.

There's Lawson, who gave me the magazines and taught me how to use the phone. 21 minutes every five hours. Sheesh!

There's the guy who met me 10 years ago at a concert backstage, Herd. He gave me some advice on how to do this time. Shit like making sure to stick to myself and creating a daily regimen to keep myself busy every day. He suggested working out, but I know my body ain't built for that.

9

There's Al, whose cell is across from mine. He's fifty something, but he acts twenty something. Reminds me of an old mafia guy.

Then there's Coach! The guy who likes guys...you know it had to be one of those. But he can and will get anything you need. I guess you can call him a "sweetheart," haha!

Now as far as the COs, there's one who really stood out. White dude. He's loud, funny, and mad cool. He would have described himself just like that. He kept it so real with me from the jump, like stay away from all these bitch-ass niggas...None of them are your friends. Him being a CO, he knew why everybody was up in this bitch. Let's just say that he pointed out all the dudes who became gangstas mysteriously overnight when they found out that I was coming...haha!

And then there's Ms. Burke. Owwwww! She's so sexy! She has a head full of gray hair, but she's not old. I'm not sure what caused it, but she said that her hair has been gray since she was thirteen. My first impression was that it's just her swag and she dyed it gray on purpose. That's how cool it looks on her. I mean, she's fine as hell. I'd definitely hit it!

Still Frustrated

Overslept for breakfast. I didn't trip because I didn't want it anyway. Woke up around eleven-ish, hit the dayroom, and had some baked chicken for chow. Yeah! It was pretty good too. I got extras and gave it to Jamaica to cook for dinner later.

It was too nasty outside for yard again, but Al and the old white guy still went. Had a visit from my manager that didn't go so well. I'm still frustrated! I just want out!

Returned to the cell around 2:45pm with well-needed new undies from one of my managers—all Polo of course! I did some writing and then hit the shower early. White was off today. Damn! Enjoyed a college basketball game in the dayroom with the fellas. Ate what Jamaica cooked, which was awesome. Read fan mail, called some back. Used up my twenty-one phone minutes too early. Went back to my cell, did some more writing, did push-ups, prayed, and listened to ESPN radio until I fell asleep.

March madness, Baby!

A bird flew into the tier...
Iggy caught it, scared all the female COs.

Still got up to get the sugar!

More Frustration

Almost overslept for breakfast again, but good ol' Al woke me up to give me sugar. He knows how much I love that sugar. Lucky me, he gave me a muffin too. He's really a good guy.

As I'm eating my muffin and sipping on my coffee, I'm thinking about how today isn't starting off so bad, considering where I am.

I shaved today thinking the girls were coming to visit, but the flight had problems. Damn!

More frustration! I just want out!

Played spades to relax my mind, won a little more than I usually do. Yeah!

Watched Celebrity Apprentice, but couldn't watch it all, had to lock in before it went off. I was still able to find out who got fired through the radio.

Did some push-ups, prayed, and fell asleep to "Yo weezy...I fuc with ya...Yo weezy...Young Mula baby!!!!" from the guy below me. Yeah!

Oh..and I'm not sore.

Someone
is always
shitting!

Fuck You, Weezy

Woke up for breakfast around 4:00 am-ish and had coffee with extra sugar of course. I went back to my cell only to fall right back asleep. Didn't wake back up until about 10:00 am-ish. No yard today because they installed seven cameras on the tier. Damn! And only on this tier. Damn! How come I feel like somebody is watching meeee?!

Then in the middle of all that, there was a cell search. It was the absolute worst. They make you strip naked, squat, and lift up ya nuts. And that's the exact way they say it... "Lift up ya nutsack!" Damn!

I had to sit and watch six officers search my cell, or should I say, mess up all my shit. They opened up all my cereal AND stomped on it. A couple of captains told me later that it wasn't supposed to happen like that. They said that there shouldn't have been more than three officers in the cell, but whatever. I guess I got that special treatment after all.

After that shit was over, we were on lockdown because of the camera installment, which lasted from 10:00am to 8:30pm. Lockdown all day. Damn!

Being that I was very up, I told my lawyer to get down here not now, but right now! He did. We spoke about what happened, and it felt good to vent.

Went back to my tier and made myself some chow. Tonight's menu was noodle soup and a Doritos burrito. Yeah! Made it myself. Charles taught me how.

Hearing my mom's voice tonight really lifted my dampened spirit. When I got back to my cell, I prayed, prayed, and prayed some more. Did some push-ups, wrote a little, and fell asleep. Bad day over! White worked tonight, which cheered me up also.

The guy below me yelled all night,
but tonight it was:

"Yo, fuck you, Weezy!"

He must have known it was a bad day...Damn!

Something Cooler

4:00am, I'm up, and coffee it is. Back out the cell at 10:00am.
Commissary Day! Yeah! Got a gang load of shit this time. I
got so much that I had to give some shit away. I gave a
full bag of shit to Charles. He didn't want to take it, but I
insisted.

We went to the yard today. I lifted some weights and shot
some ball. I must not be in the best of shape, 'cause I got
back to the cell exhausted as hell. Decided to continue a game of
spades that I'd started before going to the yard with Jamaica,
Chris, and Wilson.

Although Wilson is this old cat, he's cool. Kind of looks like
my grandma a little in the face, as if he could be her brother. I
was kicking ass in spades until I got an unexpected visit from
my lawyer. Spoke with her briefly about getting out of here
sooner than later. That went cool, but something even cooler
happened.

Big Ting escorted me back to the tier. When she saw that
I was kind of upset, she gave me some encouraging words of
wisdom. Who knew she was a sweetheart under that tough
exterior? I won't ever forget what she said: "Keep ya chin
up! You may get discouraged, but don't let it beat you @
because you'll be laughing to the bank in eight months." Yeah!

Also found out from Jamaica that "Rebirth" went gold. Yeah!
Watched American Idol with the fellas. Corny, I know, but it's

all we have. Spoke to some fans who included their phone numbers in their letters. One of them cried, which made me feel good. It was a happy cry though.

Ended the night speaking to Moms. In the midst of making myself some tea, I realized that it was too hot in the cell for that, so I made myself some Kool-Aid instead. Good thing Al showed me how to cover up the heater with a blanket or it would've felt like a sauna in this bitch all night.

Enjoyed my Kool-Aid, wrote this, did push-ups, prayed, and listened to the radio as I looked at a magazine with a girl I knew in it.

Thank God for a night without "Yo Weezy!" Yeah!

Got some cool books in the mail from a friend...Thanks, J.B.

All Smiles

I woke up in time for breakfast. Had coffee as usual only to go right back asleep. Woke up for yard and went crazy on the weights today. I got my 50 Cent on. Well, I'm probably about 35 cent, but if I stand next to 50, we almost make a dollar.

Came back to the tier to shower up early because I knew I had a visit coming soon. Having to wait for it seemed like forever, but when the visit came, it was a great visit. Three of my most precious jewels were waiting to see me: Toya, Sarah, and Niv. My loves.

All in all, the visit went well. For a couple of hours, I really appreciated being able to escape the harshness of jail.

I returned to the tier all smiles. Chris cooked tonight: lasagna, with a chicken, rice, and cheese tortilla wrap. Yeah! It's strange, but for some reason I found that shit beautiful. Played dominoes, then spades. Watched American Idol, and Human Target like it was in theaters.

Got called down to talk with mental health. She's cool, like an aunt I never had. Big Ting joked with me today again. This time it was a sexual joke about fuzzy handcuffs—OhhhW! I loved the way that she said, "Heyyy."

Also found out that the old white guy's name is Joey. He's an ex-cop and so is Al. Haha. A new inmate came on the tier today. I think his name was Cory or something. I'm not sure why, but his ass was back off the tier in minutes. He stunk anyway and was another guy that liked guys. So we named him Assistant Coach. Haha.

Dominicano was in court all day. I heard he had a fight on the way there. Crazy! Looks like he won. Yeah!

I spoke to Mack and he said they killed the performance in Mexico today. Yeah! He said Jez cried. Wow! I miss them.

After speaking to my mom, I read some fan mail, wrote this, did some push-ups, prayed, listened to ESPN, and fell asleep. Overall good day.

Another day gone. Thank God!

Oh yeah, we got a fan in the hallway now, so I can't hear the guy below me. Yeah!

And no "Damns" today. Amen!

No Place for a Gentleman

I woke up at 5am and chilled in my cell for about an hour before having coffee for breakfast. I felt like I had to take a moment to myself just to hear my own thoughts. Afterward I got a shape-up at the barbershop. The NCAA tourney started today. Yeah! Skipped yard today to watch the first game in the dayroom with Charles. I had to catch the other games on the radio during lock-in.

Man, the prison doctors have been bothering me ALL fucking day. They must think I'm either super sick or super crazy. Either way, I refused any services.

Big Ting had to escort me all day AND she was quite upset or more like frustrated for having to do so. I apologized for the inconvenience. She said it wasn't my fault. When I tried to let her walk through a door before me, she replied, "I like that ya ma taught you how to be a gentleman, but this is business." Damn!

I spoke with Flea about the suicide prevention job and hooked him up with a chick from a magazine he had. It went well and that's all I'm going to say about that, haha. Afterwards, confirmed a one-on-one basketball game with Al for July 1, his birthday.

When I got back to the tier, they were watching a DVD in the dayroom. I didn't find their movie choice too appealing, so I just went to my cell and listened to the sports station until I fell asleep.

Chris woke me up to let me know the movie was over around 8:00pm and that the game was back on in the dayroom. I filled out my bracket for the 1st round, had a few missed picks.

I cooked tonight for Jamaica and myself. Tonight's menu was rice-and-chicken tortilla wraps. Killed that shit during the game. Yeah!

A new guy hit the tier today, a young white guy who was fucking nosy, asked way too many questions, AND he fucking stunk after he got out the shower. Damn!

Spoke to Moms. Hearing her voice always brings me comfort. Also spoke to Nae. I told her that I didn't want her to come here to see me. I know that she knows that her dad is in prison, but my soul wouldn't be able to take her seeing me being led away in shackles.

Wrote this while eating some Oreos and drinking Kool-Aid. Did more push-ups, prayed, and listened to the games as I fell asleep. The combination of the game in my ear and the fan in the hallway drowned out the late-night screamers.

Another day gone. Yeah!

My First

Up at 4:00am for coffee again, with extra sugars, of course. I went to the yard today, but didn't enjoy it because the CO that was on duty bothered me the whole damn time. Talk, talk, talk. Damn! Talked the whole fucking time.

Got mail from some woman I didn't even know. She sent me some T-shirts, socks, pencils, and notebooks along with some nice pictures of herself. Yeah! I think I'll write her back. Yeah!

When I came back to the cell and wrote my first letter, it was to my daughter of course. Then I wrote to my uncle K.C. Even though it's only been 12 days since I've been in here, I can't wait until they get them.

Stepped back out into the dayroom, played spades...lost. Joey was my partner against Jamaica and Chris. I didn't eat the chow, of course-wait, yes, I did. It was chicken and veggies. Chris cooked rice and chicken, Doritos and corn. Shit was awesome! Then later Jamaica cooked chicken, rice, noodles, and lasagna. Yeah! I may get fat in here.

Ahh shit, I just saw a mouse on the tier. What the fuck am I going to do? I have way too much commissary to be letting a mouse in. Hopefully me putting my shirt under the cell door will keep that little motherfucka out my cell.

I got a two-piece today. That's a shirt and a pair of pants. I'm out of the onesie. Yeah!

I watched the tourney with Charles, Al, Dominicano, and Herd. Spoke with Mons, then Mack, then headed back to my cell for lock-in at 10:45pm. Let White hear the late-night disturbance.

23

Chris yelled back, "This ain't his cell. I'm tired of this shit!" And it kind of stopped. Thank you, Chris.

Wrote this over crackers and peanut butter. Listened to the rest of the tourney on the radio, did some push-ups, prayed, and slept.

Really looking forward to the visit tomorrow. Yeah!

Another day gone.

Put up a new picture in the cell today!

Learned a new slang today..."nice"!!

Headaches!!!

Al is shitting right now!!!

Upset City!

Got up just to have coffee for breakfast and then headed right back to the cell to go back to sleep.

I didn't get a chance to sleep that long because I was awakened at about 9:30am for a visit. I would say "damn"...but it was Lauren...so yeah! Visit went well. I miss her. She was so beautiful.

Got some new undies from E, along with a new G-Shock watch since my other one was causing so much trouble. I was told that my watch couldn't be worth over a certain dollar amount. It's not like I'm rocking an iced-out Rollie or something. It's just a simple leather-band Marc Jacobs watch. I'm sure all type of mafia mothafuckas have had way nicer watches up in the bitch. And I'm pretty sure that this was just a special Lil Wayne rule since it was implemented right after this certain bitch-ass captain asked me what type of watch I was wearing.

Had some veggies for chow before heading to the yard. Today's workout was nice. I went hard on abs and biceps. Had to get back to the dayroom to catch Villanova vs. St. Mary's. Vill lost. Upset city! Showered up, then back to the cell for lock-in at 2:45pm. Decided to spend the time reading all the mail that I received today.

Received a movie script... Damn and Yeah! First the "yeah"...It was a script for New Jack City 2, and I was to play the son of mothafucking Nino Brown! Now the "damn"...They only sent it to me in hopes that I would fund the project.

I also got a package of socks from a random fan, a letter from Lauren, and pictures of my son. Yeah! I really miss him. I accidentally dropped one of the pictures behind the heater. Damn!

I also gave E some shit to take with him just to clean my cell a little.

After doing push-ups, I headed back to the dayroom to catch Kansas vs. Iowa. Kansas lost. Upset City! Even Obama picked Kansas. Damn!

Jamaica cooked. Enjoyed that during the game. I saw Drake sitting next to Ashley Judd while watching the Kentucky game. Damn, I miss the world.

Talked to a bunch of people on the phone today...Shanell, Tez, etc. I decided to call a couple more fans. One of them wasn't home. The other one thought I was a bill collector at first, but once she realized who I was, she went bananas.

Back to the cell. Wrote, did push-ups, prayed, and fell asleep.

Another one gone!

Oh yeah, not sure if the late-night screamers are screaming...

Not listening!

Made cop jokes on Al, but I don't think he liked it too well..hahaha... fuck the police!

Cold Drinks!

Woke up too late this morning to get a razor shave. Damn! Didn't have anything else to do, so I decided to go back to sleep knowing that I had to get right back up before 10:00am. I barely made it. Got up at like 9:45-9:50am-ish. The visit from my lawyer went OK as OK can be with me still having to be in here.

I was escorted through the dorms on my way back to the tier and the inmates went crazy. I wish I were walking out instead of walking through.

Got back to the dayroom just in time for the game. No yard today because of that. Lock-in at 2:45pm. Read more of the New Jack City 2 script. I haven't finished it yet, but loving it so far!

Back out at 5:00 pm starving, so I cooked chicken, rice, and cheese tortillas. Jamaica and I killed that shit. Tried to keep my drink cold by putting it in the toilet...It worked!

Watched some good-ass basketball games. I spoke to everyone on the phone today so much that I ran out of phone time by 9:30pm. I usually never run out.

Charlie cooked dinner. He saved the baked chicken from chow earlier and cut it up or something. He had four pieces and shredded them into little pieces. Brilliant! Along with some corn, noodles, rice, and cheese. Yeah! Nice! Ate that, showered up, and watched Undercover Boss. I actually got some good ideas from it.

Before heading back to the cell, I spoke with White about how I don't listen to any music besides Young Money and about some other real shit until about 11:30pm. I got so caught up in the conversation that I have to hurry up to write this before the lights go out.

After having an apple and water for a late-night snack, I did push-ups, prayed, and listened to ESPN in the earphones.

No late-night screamers...must be asleep. Nice! Now I must.

Another day gone!

Oh yeah..Al said he's coming to one of my shows...I can't fucking wait!

Opposite World

As usual, I got up early to have coffee with plenty of sugar just to go right back to sleep. But today I got back up early enough to get a shave. Yeah!

Had a visit from the parole officer that went well. Hope it goes through. Just want out. Speaking of that, Herd was supposed to get out tomorrow but due to some reason, he isn't. Damn!

I actually ate chow today..a chicken patty. I ordered commissary with Charlie so that we have enough food for the week. Yeah!

Then I got into a confrontation with Aviles because that fool is just crazy! No biggie though. Actually everybody got into an argument with that fool today. All because he took a shower during lunchtime and afterwards came into the dayroom on some "Where's my food?" bullshit. And since Coach was serving the food, Aviles went up to him on some "Where's my food?" bullshit. Coach was like, "Yo ass was in the shower. What the fuck you want me to do, wait?"

Once we saw Coach arguing, everybody felt like they had to say something for the simple fact that Coach cleans everybody's cell. We all were like..Aviles, you tripping and shit...You ain't just going to blow up on Coach like that...You think we gonna save you some food..What's wrong with you?

Everybody was riding with Coach, but Aviles tried to go a little harder at me. Al tried to come to my rescue but I told him don't ever do that!

After that little fiasco, I went to the yard even though it was raining. It's crazy how jail can make doing what you wouldn't regularly do make sense.

I'll have to be mindful not to get lost in this opposite world.

Headed back to the cell to read the rest of the script. It was awesome!

Feeling a little claustrophobic, I hit the dayroom to finish reading mail. Got some nice mail and some crazy mail. I really enjoyed the letter from my cousin and Joe Casey. The rest were from women who sent pictures. Yeah and nice! I decided to call another fan today...she could have died!

Got another two-piece today, a fresh one, and shoes. Movies were on in the dayroom today, Inglourious Basterds. Al wanted us to be quiet, but I told him this is jail, not his living room. He didn't like that, so he went to his cell. Awww! When he came back to the tier, he was obviously upset. Sorry.

Spoke to Streets on the phone today. My nigga! My Bro! When the phones stopped working because of the rain, I played spades and learned how to play rummy or rum, whatever! Showered after I ate dinner. Charlie cooked lasagna, corn, rice, and chicken. Yeah! I'm going to get big.

Joked all night on the tier with Pacheco, another cool CO. 10:45pm rolled around, came back to the cell and wrote this, did push-ups, wrote some lyrics, prayed.

Joey found a mouse in his cell...His cell is on my side..Damn!

Another day gone!

My Sweet 16

I almost didn't wake up for coffee this morning. I got myself some extra sugars and headed back to the cell. Slept until about 10:00am. Commissary came...yeah!

Read mail all afternoon and then went to the yard. Worked out a little with Joey, Al, Chris, and Herd. Ran a lap with Chris. He actually beat me, and he's kind of on the chubby side.

Went back to the cell and wrote some lyrics. Afterwards, I went to the dayroom. It was DVD day and the first movie that we watched was The Wolfman. The second movie choice pissed me off—a freaking Tyler Perry movie...AND of course I said something about it. So when nothing was done, I headed back to my cell.

I was barely in my cell before I heard that it was shut off. It didn't make a difference at that point because I was already pissed off. Then Chris told me that they only get to watch DVDs like 3 times a month. I was like, well, we all doing time and it ain't fair to the people who didn't wanna watch. He replied, "It's about how long you've been here." Damn! So I took my little sixteen days and went to my cell.

Showered up, wrote more lyrics, did some push-ups, wrote this, and now will continue to write rhymes until the lights go off. Prayer then sleep.

Fuck it! Another day gone!

If Eminem Can

I didn't have coffee until 5:30am today. They were a little late. I went back to sleep just to get right back up to go to the barbershop. I'm fresh now.

My main focus today was calling Niv for her birthday. Called her at 8:30 this morning but wasn't able to reach her. Damn!

Then it was yard time. Hit the weights. I actually lifted 170 lbs today, 200 lbs soon. Yeah! Even Coach lifted 120 lbs twice today.

I got back to the tier super tired. My spirit was lifted somewhat when my mail came. Only downer was since the COs have to open each letter and it's so much, I have to wait for what seems like forever but it only really takes them about 15 minutes.

Oh shit, I got some of Coach's mail by mistake and there were pictures of him dressed like a girl in there...too funny! Gave Darnell some pictures I got from fans. He'll enjoy them more than me.

Showered up and Charlie cooked again...Damn...I'm going to get fat. I took a nap during lock-in at 2:45pm and was back out the cell at 5:00pm. I went straight to the phone to call Niv again. Still didn't reach her...Damn!

I was starving again so I cooked a little something for myself. Noodle soup and chicken-breast wraps, with some lettuce and carrots that I got from Joes from chow earlier. I saved it for that reason and really enjoyed it. Then I got really tired. Joked around with Chris and Charlie all day.

Idol was on the TV, but we were in the hall talking with white all night. Literally. Me, Joey, Charlie, Chris, and Jamaica.

I almost got too caught up in the conversation and forgot to call Niv again. Reached her this time. Talked to D.M.C. III, Nae Nae, and Cita too. Yeah! Also joked with Mack about some racial shit we been on all day.

Al wore a doo-rag today. He's 53 and white. Haha. He said if Eminem can wear one, so can he.

My cell feels good right now because they cut the heat back.

Wrote this, push-ups, prayer, lyrics, ESPN in the ear until I passed out.

Another day gone!

Still Got It!!!

Oh shit! I missed breakfast. Sleepyhead. Woke up at about 8:30am. Still had coffee. Jumped on the phone so my time can start. I was starving, so I cooked noodles and chicken wraps again. Ate that and then went back to the cell to sleep, but yard time came before I could thoroughly enjoy my rest. I started to pass on the yard but ended up going anyway.

The officers down there on the yard talked about how Kentucky would lose today and how Syracuse would win it all! Well, Syracuse lost! And Kentucky is up by sixteen points right now, haha. Yeah!

Shot hoops with Al. I sucked. He was much better and he's 57!

No sooner than I got back to the cell at 2:45pm, I was back out to take the test for the suicide prevention aide job. I passed with a 100, no lie. Guess I still got it. And I guess I still get that mula baby, because S.P.A. is the highest-paying job an inmate can get. The job is basically to monitor the tier for an eight-hour shift and if someone wants to hang up (meaning to kill themselves), to not negotiate with them or try to talk them out of it, but just to alert an officer. You get paid $50 if you stop the person from actually hanging themselves and $25 if you find them hung up. Yeah, it's that real.

When I got back to the cell, I wrote some rhymes and did some push-ups until about 4:30. Ended up playing checkers with Dominicano, Lost!

Then I had to get ready for my visit, which was Tez, Mack, and E.I. That was a great visit. I told them about everything I've gone through since being here. I miss them niggas. We talked for about an hour and a half. I hated to have to end it but had to cut the visit short when seven o'clock came around so I could get back for the game. Did that just in time.

Had chow when I got back. It was this chicken special that Coach and LL make. Shit is great! Also made my own rice and noodles with it and put it on a tortilla wrap. Shit was awesome. I feel fat. Watched the games attentively.

Used the phone cautiously. Spoke to my little man D.M.C. III, he said "Dada." Fucked up that I had to hear it for the first in here but still, yeah!

Showered up quickly then had tea which I'm still drinking now. It's 10:45pm and I'm back in my cell listening to a game in the earphones as I write this.

Push-ups, prayer, sleep.

Another day gone!

                        Side note: Saw Drake by Ashley Judd again and found out that the coach is flying him to the games...damn.

Jailhouse Rap

Got up just for coffee, then headed right back to the cell to sleep. I woke back up at 9:00 am but didn't leave the cell until about 9:30am.

Jumped right on the phone and talked a bit. Then read fan mail. Got some nice pictures today and Marisa sent me some Marc Jacobs cashmere socks—Yeah!

Some people write the most bugged-out things. Everything from wanting to fall asleep with my dick in their mouth, to "I rep my city astronomically!" Crazy, man! I love it! Also read the new Rolling Stone and I was in it. Yeah!

Hunger pains started to kick in, so I made chicken and noodle wraps. Yard came around. I went and got a great workout. I talked smack with the cap and CO about the games last night. I also got some new boots today.

I rapped for the first time on the yard for Charlie and Jamaica. It's crazy that I've performed in front of millions of people since I was eight years old, but for some reason I was nervous as hell. Rapping has always been second nature to me, but my creativity has definitely been put to the test since being in this bitch. I absolutely refuse to rap about being in jail. It's not who I am AND it's not who I'm going to be! I hope they liked it. I think they did.

I made it back to the tier at about 1:30pm. Locked in at 2:45pm as usual. Wrote some lyrics, did some push-ups, and read some more mail. Back out at 4:30pm.

Chris gave me two bags of Doritos. I gave him some bubblegum.

It wasn't a trade, just two generous guys. But, yeah, someone blessed me with some gum, a Now & Later, and a Jawbreaker today. Yeah!

Games came on at 7:00 pm. Tuned in...pretty good competition...I enjoyed it. Penn won! It's the first time they advanced past the Sweet 16 in school history—yay for them! Charlie cooked rice, corn, lasagna, chicken, and noodles for dinner just in time to enjoy during the game.

Called some fans today...They greatly appreciated it. In all honesty, I did too. It was one of the highlights of my day, next to speaking to my beautiful daughter, who was at the hair salon. She's so grown.

Showered..White worked tonight...Yeah!

Spoke to Moms at 10:00 pm. Locked in at 10:45 pm. Wrote this over a Doritos burrito and some Nestea.

Push-ups, prayer, ESPN, sleep.

Oh yeah, found out how to make air freshener by peeling an orange and setting it in the toilet with urine. Damn, but Yeah.

Another day gone!

Side note: Coach said he was
going to braid my hair tomorrow.

She Got Balls

Up for coffee and then back to the cell. Slept until about 8:30am, when Palmer woke me up for a visit...an attorney visit that I didn't know about. The first thing I thought was this can only be one of two things...something bad has happened for them to pop up on me without warning me, or I'm going home, because they are always fighting to get me up out this bitch. So of course I focus on the positive like...oh shit...an attorney visit out of the blue... I'm going home... I'm about to leave this bitch!

So when I got to the attorney visitation area, all I saw was hair and I was thinking, That ain't my attorney. I was really confused until she looked up and I realized that it was this girl I know who's an attorney. I couldn't help but smirk thinking about how this bitch said she was going to do this shit. As soon as I sat down, I was like, Wow...you bold...but I like that in you. She was shaking like crazy while holding her fake papers and folders.

We kicked it, talked, laughed, and joked. She asked me how it was in here and I asked her what she's been up to. She told me that she got a new ass.

So after the visit, I was filled with a mixture of disappointment that I wasn't leaving and being pleasantly surprised by her visit. The escorting captain must have sensed more disappointment and told me, "Don't worry, this time shall pass and you'll be even bigger and better. You're making millions now, maybe it'll be billions later!" Shit, I hope!

Came back to the tier hungry, so I cooked chicken, noodles, and cheese rice! Shit was awesome. Didn't go to the yard, had a splitting headache all day. Took a trip to the clinic today once the nurse felt my pounding headache. That trip was quick though. The nurse and doctors are cool. We spoke about New Orleans and things. Took some medicine before taking a nap. It went away by the time I woke up, which was at 5:00pm, just in time to catch the last game. Butler beat K. State. I picked K. State. Damn! Spoke to Drake on the phone, told him we saw him at the Kentucky games, but he said he wouldn't be at the game tonight and they lost. I picked Kentucky. Damn!

Dinner was great. Charlie cooked. Same ol', same ol', but it tasted wonderful.

Back to the tier, joked with White. Did some reading. The 48 Laws of Power, enjoying it, and more mail. Also got more mail today...more nice pics as well...yeah!

Showered up, but not before Coach braided my hair. Did a cool job given the fact we don't have any hair products.

Phone and more phone. Told E to tell Tez to get me that new Land Rover that I saw in a commercial today. All black should be waiting for me when I get out.

Tomorrow can't get here fast enough...Moms is coming...Yeah!!!

Lock-in at 10:45pm.

Wrote this, push-ups, prayer, ESPN, sleep.

Another day gone!

(Actually listening to a gospel station...love it!)

The Best Day so far

Up for coffee at 5:00am and then back to the cell to sleep.
I didn't wake back up until 10:00am. Had more coffee. I knew
Mom landed at 10:00am, so I called E. He said they were waiting
for the shuttle, so I got prepared as well.

They called me down for my visit right after chow, which I did eat.
It was chicken and veggies. Then it was time to see Moms. Had
to wait about ten minutes before she actually showed up. It felt
like forever. Guess they brought me down a little early. We hugged
super tight when she did get there. Seeing her let me know how
much I missed her smile.

She was like, "They treating you right up in here? You eating? You
not getting into any fights, right?" Emotionally I was weak because
I didn't ever want my mom to see me like this, but she gave me the
strength to stay strong. My mom is so tough. I love her so much!

This by far was my best day already. We continued to talk about
everything from being in here to Samas, my little brother. She told
me that he wants to be a rapper now. Yeah! But he's also playing
soccer and swimming now too. He's an all-around sports kid—football,
baseball, and now this. I love it!

She wanted to know who did my hair. I told her Coach...hahaa...We
laughed. E brought my glasses finally. We rambled on and on about
how it is in here and how it is out there. I had to pee bad
as hell and I knew I only would be able to do it in my cell, so we
wrapped it up with another tight hug and kiss. I told her it
was the best visit so far. She was happy to see me, but I
could tell she was sad to leave and that got me a little upset,
but she was still cool. It was hard for me to handle seeing her
going to the right as I went to the left after spending time
with her. It's the absolute worst part of a visit. To have to

Watch my mom, or whoever, leave, always takes my spirits down. They leave and I have to go back to Cell 29 in handcuffs and shackles on my feet.

As soon as I got back to the cell, I headed straight to the toilet. Then I made me a Ruffles-and-noodle burrito to enjoy during lock-in. The game was on the radio and Tennessee lost. Damn.

Back out at 5:00pm. Phone then dayroom but it was so loud on the tier, I almost stayed in my cell. But of course when the next game came on, I stayed and watched it with the fellas. Baylor lost. Damn! I hate Duke.

Charlie cooked. But my man LL made me a nice rice, chicken, and veggie dish as well. I ate both. I'm going to be fat.

After the game, the fellas wanted to watch 60 Minutes. Lame! Then it was DVD time, but the movie was The Surrogates. Lame! We watched that shit until 10:00pm. Al got mad because some of us were talking during the movie, which made us talk even louder, haha. He was pissed. And when he went to his cell, Dominicano kept asking the CO to turn off his cell light and he did. Haha. That shit was too funny. We watched Undercover Boss at 10:00pm and again I got some ideas.

Spoke with a CO to kill time. He told me that he had been here for 20 years and was about to retire soon. And how there are some inmates that he saw on his first day still here... Damn!

Made some more coffee, locked in at 10:45pm.

Wrote this, push-ups, lyrics, prayer, ESPN, sleep.

Al's shitting right now.

Another day gone!

Started reading this book today called Scar Tissue
by Anthony Fiedis from the Red Hot Chili Peppers.
Good book so far...he's a crazy guy.

Damn...I'm Really in Jail

Got up to have my morning coffee as normal. I couldn't go back to sleep due to a terrible migraine, which I feel like is coming back now as I write this, so this will be short. Waited what felt like a lifetime for my meds. Got them, took them, headache went away. Thank God. Cooked my own lunch: noodle, chicken, and cheese rice on a tortilla again.

It rained today, so I didn't go to the yard. We watched Planet of Terror on DVD—another movie with Bruce Willis in it. Yesterday was The Surrogates—he's in that as well. Locked in 2:45pm, of course. Had another headache unfortunately.

Got more mail today and some awesome pictures. Read some of the mail during lock-in. Cool shit. I love my peeps. Joe and Feuk's letters made me laugh. Tara and Amy's made me feel loved. Someone unknown sent me a $20 money order—how cool! I hope commissary is tomorrow.

Back out the cell. Pecheco was working tonight. He's cool. He brought a DVD, which was Cop Out, another Bruce Willis movie! It was cool.

Spoke with Mack and he told me I could start writing for ESPN. How fucking cool! Yeah!

Read more of Scar Tissue. Dancing with the Stars was on after the movie. Charlie cooked today. I traded a coffee pack for a pack of noodles. Damn...I'm really in jail!

Showered up. Kind of tired so I headed to my cell early. Damn, my head is really starting to hurt again. Took two Tylenols, hope they work.

Wrote this, few push-ups, prayer, listened to some gospel, and then sleep. Wait, Flea just tossed me a magazine with girls in it. Going to check that out first, then sleep.

And another one gone!

(My sink is stopped up, damn.)

Don't Know Why or How

Woke up at 6:30am, so I missed the morning chow. Had coffee at 10:00am because I went back to sleep. My head killed me all night and all day. Cluster migraine, the worst. Actually I have one right now. Don't know why or how I'm writing this. I'm about to make myself a Doritos burrito for lunch.

Went to yard even though it was nasty out. A little rain but I figured since I didn't go for the past two days, I should.

Read more mail and Scar Tissue. Afterwards, I played spades with Charlie, Chris, and Jamaica. Lost.

Idol was on. Crystal Bowersox merked it.

Showered up. My head is still killing me.

I'm back in my cell, no writing...just prayer and sleep. Damn.

Another one.

The Switch-Up

Woke up early as usual for my morning coffee. Wanted to switch it up, so I had Rice Krispies for breakfast today. Got extra sugar from my dude who looks out for me every morning. Ms. Reid blessed me as well. Yeah!

Middleton clocked in, looking tired as usual. He reminded us that there would be no hot water from 8am to 8pm, so if we wanted to shower early, do so. I just shaved instead because I had to look fresh for my visit today.

Headed back to the cell with my coffee in me. No cuffs today on the way back to the cell, cool captain. Got some more tees and boxers as usual from E. He's unbelievably great!

It was almost chow time when I returned to the tier, but I jumped on the phone with a few people before I ate. It was like some turkey stew or something. Surprisingly it was good though.

Afterwards I played spades with Charlie, Jamaica, and Wilson. Won! Wrote a letter to a friend and spoke with Mack. Watched Idol. Charlie cooked lasagna and chicken wraps. Enjoyed that too.

Got more mail along with some more great pictures too. Yeah! I joked around in the dayroom before getting back on the phone with my babies' mothers. Afterwards, hit the dayroom and did more joking around. Took my meds. Refused mental health conversation. The mental-health lady was mad because she likes to talk to me. Lock-in came. White worked tonight, by the way, so that's a plus.

Wrote this, push-ups, prayer, thank God I don't have a headache, ESPN, sleep.

And a-fucking-nother 1 gone!

1st Night on the Job

Woke up, had coffee and some cereal, and then back to sleep. Back up at 10:00am with a headache. Damn! I had no choice but to call for meds, got 'em, felt a little better. I wasn't feeling too hungry so I passed on chow. Went to the yard and got a good workout. Triceps, biceps, and abs. Oh yeah, and obliques — I think that's how you spell that. They're sore now. Spoke with the officers about sports as usual.

Then back to the tier to clean myself up a bit. Had some tea. Spoke to Flea about his S.P.A. job because tonight will be my first night on the job, uh-oh. He told me I have nothing to worry about. Just check the cells every thirty minutes and when the captain passes, always stand. Piece of cake, I hope.

Locked in at 2:45, of course. Headache, damn! Took a million Tylenols, helped a little. Back out at 5:00. White was working, yeah. But today is his last day before his vacation, damn.

I think Idol was on — yeah, it was. I think. Attacked the phone so much I ran out of minutes, damn. Didn't even get to call Moms.

Charlie cooked. Ate and enjoyed. Showered up. Chatted it up with White, Jamaica, Herd, and Flea on his last night as well. Flea gets out tomorrow morning. I'm happy for him like I'm getting out. Yeah, Flea. Don't come back! Ever!

Lock-in time came, but since I'm S.P.A. now I don't lock in at 10:45 anymore. I stay out until 6:00am. This will be interesting. Everyone locked in. I did my first check of the cells, which is called a tour. Set up two chairs by my cell, which stays open now, and read Scar Tissue. White clocked out, Medina clocked in. 12:00am came — another day gone! But I'm still up on the job. Work!
I'm planning on spending most of my shift posted up outside my cell

and just walking the tier every 15 minutes to see if anybody needs anything. Since everybody else is locked in at 10:45pm. I might have to bring somebody some water, have the CO cut off somebody's light, or something else simple like that. I don't have to do shit like that, but I don't have a problem doing extra.

Hope I make it.

(You should see me with my little flashlight and all, haha.)

I Now Pronounce You

Been up all morning on the job. It's been a pretty easy workday. Nobody was hanging up in their cell. Thank God! I'm super tired though. I did everything to stay up, from reading to writing to what felt like a billion push-ups until my body couldn't take any more. I went to get my morning coffee only thinking about getting back to the cell to sleep. Nothing much to do now but count the minutes until my shift is over at 6:00am. 6:00am came and so did the sleep. I have no idea why, but woke right back up at 10:30am.

Yard was early today at, like, 11:00am. Asked Charlie if he was going, he said no, so I passed as well. I think I jumped on the phone. Tennis and golf were being watched, surprisingly, in the dayroom. Then lock-in came. Slept straight through that.

Woke back up at 4:30pm, back out the cell to jump back on the phone. The Final Four was on at 6:30pm. I watched the first game. Butler amazingly won...damn! I was going for Michigan State.

I fixed myself a nice dinner during the second half. Charlie helped me finish it. Took another nap after the first game. Even though I was super tired from the job, I found the energy to come back out to enjoy the rest of it, but jumped back on the phone for most of it instead. Duke won.

Lock-in time for everybody else, job time for me. Middleton clocked in. I pulled up a chair by Jamaica and Charlie's cell and chatted it up with them for about an hour. We joked with Coach about his new marriage to Dominicano that happened yesterday. Coach is always fuckins with Dominicano about him being his man and shit. Being that Dominicano is so Dominican and don't understand too much English, he doesn't know that we be fucking with him. Coach said that he wanted to marry Dominicano and put on a white sheet like it was a dress. Niggas were pushing Dominicano up to our makeshift altar. He didn't know what was going on and was like, "What are you doing, man? What are you doing, man?" When they got him to the back, I married them.

I got the Bible and I'm like, we gathered here today. Dominicano didn't know what the fuck was going on until I got to the "I now pronounce you." He was like, "Fuck that, man. No, fuck that, man." We threw rice and shit. We hung tissue paper up around the day room. We wrote "Coach and Dominicano" all around the dayroom. We even had a reception, which everybody brought something for the couple. I brought cookies since Coach loves cookies. But when that nigga Chris brought 10 Gatorades, it went down in this bitch. Gatorade is liquid gold in this bitch. We all were like, OOOOH SHIT...It's going dooooWWWnnn!

For the music, everybody was running about that bitch with headphones listening to the same station straight up jamming! Coach sat in his chair as everybody walked up to give him his gifts. And to top things off, Coach wrapped up a pillowcase like it was a bundle, cut out a face from a magazine, and put it on it like it was a real baby. That shit was too funny! Imagine seeing grown-ass men in jail hanging tissue for wedding decorations...AND one of them is Lil Wayne...Crazy!

After we all had a good laugh, I went back to my post, which is in front of my cell, and began the night on the job by reading more Scar Tissue.

Twelve o'clock came, another day gone.

Jailhouse Cliché

Woke up at 10:00am to the sound of Iggy saying, "Commissary!" Commissary on a Monday? Yeah! I filled out my list, making sure not to forget anything this time. They still didn't have everything I put on the list, but that's OK though. I got more than enough shit. Al had given me a pack of coffee earlier, but I gave him two packs when commissary came.

Wieners and beans for lunch—I passed. Went to yard instead and had a good chest and triceps work out. Back to the tier and had a Doritos burrito with tea. Didn't lock in because I worked the 2-10 shift again. Same CO from yesterday showed up, damn. I don't like him. It was already kind of cold on the tier and he turned on the fan. We didn't complain about it though. We just turned it off.

I fixed myself another Doritos burrito with a beef stick this time before jumping on the phone. I couldn't imagine being in here without having a daily connection with the outside world. I know it sounds like a typical jailhouse cliché, but my appreciation for the multiple blessings in my life has grown tenfold since being locked up in this bitch.

I got called down to the clinic to get my blood and blood pressure checked. For what reason I don't know, but didn't have a choice, so away I went. Captain Henton (Big Ting) is a comedian. She threatened to pull my dreads out, haha. The CO in the bubble who patted me down thought I called her "baby" when I clearly said "ma'am." She probably wanted me to say "baby."

Showered up. Dancing with the Stars was on. Got on the phone for about 25 minutes straight with this special someone. Yeah!

Got more fan mail, read some and responded. Also got a letter from Sarah's mom and Joe Casey. Joked with Jamaica, Dominicano, Charlie, and Chris until lock-in.

Wrote this listening to Nicki on some reggae shit. Killing it! I love my team. Can't wait to get back in the game.

Push-ups, rhymes, prayer, ESPN, sleep.

Another one gone!

Don't Act Like

When I found out that Harrington had AIDS, I couldn't help but to look at him differently. I don't wish that shit on no man, whether friend or foe. But any feelings of empathy that I had for him left after he went off on me today.

It all started from me noticing this crazy-ass smell that was coming from his cell. As the suicide prevention aide, I sat outside my cell from 10pm to 6am...I'm cell 29 and he's cell 28...and that's a long-ass time to smell a funky-ass odor.

I'm like, what the fuck is this dude doing to make his cell stink like this? Then it clicked: dude don't ever take showers. I mean, as hot as it's been up in this bitch, I've never seen him take one freaking shower. So since he was cool with Coach and Coach is my dude, I pulled Coach to the side and was like, I know y'all cool and shit...why don't you tell him on the low to jump in the shower or something?

And Coach was like, "I be telling her to take a damn shower. She don't ever want to get in that damn shower. I tell her ass that every time." And I'm like, well can you tell her ass again, because a nigga starting to smell her ass and it ain't popping. I couldn't help but to laugh a little at how crazy it sounds for us to be talking about a man like we're talking about a woman.

I guess Coach must have told him exactly what I said in the midst of telling him. So Harrington comes into the dayroom and just goes off on me. "You mothafucka...Don't tell me to take no fucking shower. You don't tell me when to take a shower. I'm a grown-ass man and I ain't got to get in the fucking shower. And you think I don't know about you. I've already read the articles. You think I don't know you a druggie...You're just a junkie!"

He starts going in on how I'm a junkie and how I'm addicted to cough syrup. "You think I don't know you a junkie? You ain't perfect, you ain't special, trying to tell me to take a shower."

I was like, Wow, dude! Because Harrington is old, I really didn't want to say anything back to him, plus I knew he had AIDS. Then he starts fussing at more than just me when other people started saying stuff like, 'Nah, Harrington, you really do be stinking, my nigga...You really do need to take your ass to the shower."

That's when Harrington took that shit to a whole nother level and started talking about everybody in this bitch...straight exposing niggas. He told Al, "Don't act like I don't know what you be doing back there...Don't act like I don't know you be back there jacking Chris off. Explain that!"

Everybody was like, "OH MY GOD, what the fuck is this?!" I was more like, Thank you, because the weight shifted off of me about being a druggie and he exposed someone else. After that, they packed his bags and shipped him off. Their main thing is protecting Carter...They have to protect Carter, and Carter can't get into any arguments, no nothing...because I could sue.

What a day...but at least it's another one gone!

Burrito Party

Woke up at 10:30am and had myself some coffee. I came right back to my cell because I didn't want to watch Wendy Williams. I tried to write, but didn't come up with much though. Back to the tier with my tablet just in case I do think of some shit. Found out that there won't be yard today because there was a stabbing in another building. Welcome to Jail.

Doritos burrito time! Charlie had showed me how to add a beef jerky stick in my shit a couple of days ago. Shit is great! Lock-in came and I jumped back into bed. Woke up about 6:40-ish and back out the cell at 7:00. Then back in the cell at 7:30 to rest up more because I'm working the night shift. Back out at 8:30, straight to the phone. Then showered up. Idol was on. Everybody was eating a Doritos burrito. We called it a burrito party. I jumped back on the phone until 10:45. They locked in and I posted up by Charlie's cell. Ended up talking to him and Jamaica until 1:00 a.m.

Medina came in smelling like a bucket of cologne. I went through fan mail and then wrote this. Medina just gave me some sugars, my G. Doing some push-ups to stay up. Passed on breakfast, it was hot whole grain wheat cereal, yuck. I settled for an apple and coffee. Got to slow down on the sugar.

I'm bumping in the earphones right now, but I'm about to write some of my own rhymes. Sharell is coming to visit tomorrow, so I got to shave in the morning. Before I write rhymes, I have to write a foreword for Toya's book.

Al's farting and Joey is coughing. Jail!

Wrote some lyrics, going to pray, read the Bible, and zzzzz.

Another one.

(I learned how to make air freshener with a nasal-spray bottle, shampoo, and water. It actually works.)

Neatly Folded Boxers

Woke up at 9:30 to shave then right back to sleep. I woke back up at 1:30 and jumped on the phone until it was time for my visit. Damn...Shanell looked so fucking good! Had a great visit with her. She said it was weird to see me like that. I understand. Damn... I miss my team!

I got back to the tier after two hours. Nothing much was on going in the dayroom, so I straightened up and chilled in my cell until about 5:00. Even made myself a Doritos burrito with the beef jerky—no surprise, right?! Jumped on the phone, and then back to bed from 6:30–8:30.

I woke up to the smell of what Jamaica was cooking. I ate some of that shit and then jumped back on the phone before showering up. Hit the dayroom to watch Idol...It's elimination day. Then more phone, more phone, more phone.

Had a funny jailhouse moment when Jamaica locked Coach in Dominicano's cell and locked Dominicano in Coach's cell. And when Coach started to neatly fold Dominicano's boxers, we all could've died from laughing...Shit was too funny!

Right before lock-in, I told Coach I was going to need my hair braided tomorrow.

It's lock-in for everyone else, but punch-in time for me. I started my shift posted up by Charlie's cell. Talked to him and Jamaica until 1:30am. Found out that Charlie's daughter is five-years old, and Jamaica has an eighteen-year-old and a twenty-one-year-old daughter by an Englishwoman. Interesting.

I posted up by my cell and started to write this. Medina just gave me some sugars, my G. It's 2:00am right now as I'm listening to T.I. on the radio. Fuck, still got 4 hours left before I'm able to go to sleep. Decided to do more push-ups before having an apple and coffee for breakfast. Joey and Herd ate the grits and PB&J sandwiches. They eat PB&J sandwiches with whatever is for breakfast. I don't get it.

These little fucking ants are every damn where! They're really pissing me off. It's probably the reason why Medina sterilizes everything before he touches it...and he wears gloves to close the cells, haha.

Wrote some nice rhymes.

Prayer, Bible, ESPN, zzz.

Another one!

All This for Her

I woke up at noon, shaved and then headed straight to the phone. I didn't go to yard because I was just waking up. Had a visit that went very well.

When I got back to the tier, LL had made some chicken, rice, and veggies. Shit was good! Showered up afterwards. The Yankees game came on and of course everybody in here is a Yankees fan. Not me!

Quit S.P.A. job today. I'd rather just do my time. I'm eating Oreos and drinking grape KoolAid as I write this right now. This is the kind of shit that has become worth writing about: eating Oreos and drinking grape KoolAid. Damn!

I'm getting sleepy, so I'm about to nap.

Woke back up at 10:35 and headed straight to the phone before lock-in. Jamaica is S.P.A. now. He just brought me some hot water and even though I'm still very tired...Doritos burrito time!

Got a big day tomorrow because I'm having a visit from a new friend, awww!!! Coach braided my hair. Hope she likes it. I'm going to take them out in the morning so my hair can be curly. All this for her.

Charlie just asked if my friend has a sister and Coach asked if she has a brother! Hahaha. Crazy.

I was going to try to write some rhymes but the lights went out just as I was checking out the new issue of Rolling Stone. Damn!

Nothing for me to do now but push-ups, prayer, Bible, sleep.

Another one gone.

Damn, Damn, Damn

I woke up this morning around 9-something. I couldn't leave the cell though. We were on lockdown because somebody got stabbed. I tried to go back to sleep but got woke back up at 9:30 am for mail. Got my mail and then took my ass straight back to sleep. Woke back up about 11:30 for more mail. I decided to stay up after that.

Hopped on the phone to see what time my visit was coming. One o'clock felt like an eternity away. Watched Power Rangers to pass the time instead of going to yard. Time for my visit eventually came. First had to take out my braids...hair curly...Yeah!

Went down with Captain Gunn, who is pretty cool. He let me take my rap folder down. Mack, Baby, and my new friend, Nikki, were waiting for me. Had a marvelous visit, although I had to pee the whole time. She was looking amazing. Black top, gray tights, black boots...damn, damn, damn!

Back to the tier with my man White and Mack, who just happened to be walking up at the same time. Glad White is back...that's my dude.

The NBA play-offs started today. Yeah! Missed the first half because we were locked in. Damn! Passed the time by doing some push-ups and writing rhymes. Can't stop thinking about how freaking good Nikki looked today. Damn, she's bad! Luckily I was able to catch the second half. Cavs won. Jumped on the phone with some fans, showered, and hit the dayroom to watch Clash of the Titans.

Ended the night by watching some MMA fights and a baseball game that went into the fifteenth inning and listening to the NBA play-offs in my earphones.

Herd ate a meal fit for three people...no, actually for five people.

When I got back to my cell for lock-in, I did some push-ups and sorted through fan mail. Jamaica is working S.P.A. tonight and he just made soup for us. I also had some Rice Krispies.

Read some Tao Te Ching, prayer, Bible, ESPN, sleep.

Another one.

(Side note: We were all jamming to the radio until Middleton came and said we were making too much noise.)

Rhyme Time

I woke up later than usual this morning, at 9:50. I shaved, made some phone calls, and then headed straight back in my cell to sleep by 10:50. Woke back up when they called for chow but didn't eat because LL is cooking his special tonight.

By that time, yard came. I decided to go and ended up having a great workout on my chest, triceps, back, and oblique. When I got back to the tier, I read and responded to some fan mail. During lock-in, I listened to the Lakers game on the radio before doing push-ups and reading and responding to more mail.

White came in with some sugars for me-my dude! Mack and Pecheco are working again as well. Should be a good day. It has been so far.

As soon as lock-in ended, I went to the dayroom to catch the rest of the Lakers game. Beforehand, I jumped on the phone, of course. I spoke to my daughter. She's absolutely amazing and growing up so fast. D.M.C. III is always eating. Kam had just woken up from a nap.

There was a good game going on. Ron Artest's hair is crazy! Lakers won. Tough game but expected. Starving, finally ate. Food was good. Then came Rhyme time...

I started reading and responding to more mail before heading back to my cell for lock-in. Right now I'm eating cereal out of an old peanut-butter jar. Mini Wheats. Extra sugar because them shits are nasty without. Chris is working S.P.A. White just turned everyone's lights out, joking around. We all were screaming at the same time, "LIGHTS!" Al said he was on the toilet and he couldn't see! I've been singing this Spanish song all day I learned from Dominicano. "La Cucaracha, La Cucaracha"...haha!

I'm going to write some rhymes, do some push-ups, maybe read and respond to more mail, pray, Bible, and call it a night.

Another one.

(Iggy has a MMA fight tonight. Hope he kicks ass.)

What She Said

Woke up at 4:30am for breakfast. Had cereal and coffee before going back to sleep until about 11-something. I was up for the day, so I headed to the dayroom. I passed on lunch and just had more coffee instead. My morning phone time was cut short all of sudden because we had to lock in. Damn! They said somebody was missing from another building. I hope he got away!

Luckily for me, they delivered my mail during lock-in...and lots of it! Yeah! I love my fans! I read as much as I could before yard. Got another nice workout in. Felt tight afterwards though. Since yard was kind of late due to the earlier lock-in, we came back to the tier at 245pm, which is lock-in time as well. Damn!

Went through more mail during that time. White came on the job. Look out. Hit the dayroom with a gang of mail. Then out of the blue they called for commissary. Yeah! Filled out my list, then they called for linen exchange. LL cooked a special dish...Shit was good! Showered.

When I went to put my commissary up, the light in my cell wasn't working. We tried and tried but no luck. This is some bullshit. I'm going to have to spend the night in the dark. Damn! Jumped on the phone and watched a little of Dancing with the Stars. Wasn't that much into it, so I chatted it up with White until lock-in. I tried to fuck with the light again, but still nope. So now I'm in the dark writing this. I got a lot of candy, chips, and cookies though, so I'll be straight. Plus I talked to my daughter and she said to smile no matter what. I miss her badly!

Rhymes, push-ups, prayer, Bible, snacks, ESPN, zzzz.

It's too damn dark...Another one gone! (Jamaica's working tonight... better him than me.)

Never Ever Ever

Woke up for breakfast, had Mini Wheats and coffee. Ms. Reid called me "Shotta" like Jamaica does when she gave me extra sugars. I like the way she said it much better. After breakfast, it's back to cell to sleep 'til about 8:30 am...didn't want to miss the opportunity to get a share AND complain about my light not working. Also had to call Tez to tell him to build a studio and gym at my house. With all three missions accomplished, the only thing left to do now is to go back to sleep. I wished I could've slept longer, but woke right back up at 11:00 with a headache...It's 11:38 and it's still aching...Damn! Bad start to hopefully a good day.

Couldn't let the headache allow me to do nothing, so I read some mail and wrote some rhymes. In the midst of my headache-induced writing session, the feeling of missing my kids overwhelmed me. It made me even more determined to never put myself in a situation like this again...never, ever, ever!

The Price Is Right was on in the dayroom. I tried to play along, but just kept thinking about how this place is wrong. Lock-in rolled around, so I headed back to my cell to read and respond to fan mail. Finally maintenance came to fix my light, but come to find out it's the circuit, not the bulbs. Still broken...jail...Damn! Came back to the cell to read and respond to more mail. Charlie cooked. Shit was good.

I just showered up and made myself some tea to drink while listening to the Mets game on the radio. Idol is on in the dayroom. Jamaica, Chris, and Wilson are playing poker for fifty cents, Al's talking shit, and Dominicano is cleaning. I'm about to make a burrito ...yeah...another burrito.

Chris is working, but my light isn't. I ain't tripping though: it's blinking on and off like a disco, so it's like I'm in the club. About to listen to my radio, clubbing, slow jams are on, even better.

Chris just threw water into Dominicano's cell. He's pissed, but so what...He told the CO...and we don't do that!

About to write some more rhymes, push-ups, prayer, Bible, sleep.

Another one.

People Play Too Much

Woke up this morning, had some coffee, and headed straight to the phone. Came back to my cell mad as hell because of an argument that I just had on the phone. They finally fixed the light in my cell, so hopefully that's a sign that the day will get better. Being that I wasn't in the best of moods, I just went back to sleep and didn't wake back up until they called for yard. Didn't go... made a burrito and listened to my radio in the dayroom instead. I got called to the clinic for a checkup. Everything is perfect.

It's lock-in time right now and I'm in my cell going through fan mail and doing push-ups. Pacheco is the CO on post now. The day is getting better so far. I think I'll write some rhymes. Yeah, it's rhyme time!

It's 11:13pm and I'm back in my cell. I played dominoes with Charlie and Dominicano during lock-out. Charlie cooked...shit was good. Idol was good today too. Joked with Pacheco...That kid is hilarious. He has this whistle that he blows while he dances...Too funny!

Called a fan who has been sending me these five-to-seven-page letters that seemed as if she thought she knew me or met me. When I spoke to her, she told me that someone told her that they were me on Myspace a while back. People play too much. She was upset when I told her it wasn't me, but happy to hear from the real me.

I'm doing push-ups now and listening to music. Jamaica made soup...Yeah...about to enjoy that. Oh yeah, Jamaica is working obviously. Reading mail and responding.

It's 12:00am lights just went out. Today turned out not to be so bad after all. Another one gone!

25 More

Woke up for breakfast...had Rice Krispies and coffee. Couldn't go back to sleep, had too much on my mind, so I just chilled in my cell until I was able to use the phone at 8:30.

I eventually was able to go back to sleep until around 11:00. It didn't really matter because we were still on lockdown. Back to sleep it was, then, woke back up at noon, still on lockdown...Damn!

Then Ms. Burke came to my cell and told me to get dressed. I thought it was for my visit, but it was for a drug test. I went down...pissed in a cup...came back clean...Yeah!

When I got back to the tier, we were still on lockdown. We didn't get out of lockdown until 4:30pm. No visit. Well, Baby, Mack, and Nicki came, but couldn't see me due to the lockdown. Damn!

I told Captain Armstrong I wanted to change cells because of ants. So now I'm in Cell 11, which is right across from my old cell. It's much cleaner and no ants. And I don't have to deal with the loud guy who sings Spanish songs all day and night under Cell 29 anymore. Yeah!

Somebody brought in new movies today, not sure who, but I think it was Pecheco. We watched Shutter Island. It was cool!

It's 10:01pm and I'm about to get on the phone.

I just got off the phone and I'm fresh out the shower. Lock-in time. I'm writing this and doing push-ups...300 of them. Going to write some rhymes before the lights go out. Jamaica is working again tonight. He just gave me hot water for tea. Jamaica makes way too much noise as S.P.A. I don't think he will have the job long. Palmer was the CO, back from vacation. He's cool. Rhyme time. Lights just went off.

Prayer, 25 more push-ups, Bible, ESPN, zzzzzzzzzzz.

Visit tomorrow. Another one.

Too Much of Nothing

Up at 9:30am to shave and then headed straight back to sleep. The days seem to get longer and longer, with absolutely nothing to do at all. Whoever thinks that jail is cool is outta their fucking mind. I even feel sorry for the COs who have to be in here, but not too sorry though—at least they get to go home every night.

I managed to get back up at noon for yard, I'm glad I did because I had a nice workout. When I got back up to the tier around 1:30, I made a burrito and watched America's Funniest Home Videos with Charlie.

Made some calls and now I'm back in my cell for lock-in...It's only 2:48pm. See what I mean? Days spent doing too much of fucking nothing.

As I sat and waited for my visit, I made myself some tea, read some mail, and listened to the draft on the ESPN radio station. Charlie was working. He's really a cool dude.

My visit was great...It really helped break the monotony of this long-ass day.

Now I'm in the dayroom watching UFC fights, about to get on the phone.

Back in the cell for lock in...It's 1:02am. Lights been off for an hour, but I found this new slow-jam station on the radio, so I've been doing push-ups and dancing all night. I'm jamming...but only for a few

More minutes though.. I'm abart to be asleep like a baby.

I wrote a fan from Sweden back when I first locked in. A cutie!

More push-ups, prayer, Bible, out!

Another one.

Survey Says

Woke up at 10-something for mail then right back to sleep until 12:30. Jumped on the phone, made a burrito, and read the paper...the sports section of course.

I couldn't stand having nothing better to do than watch Family Feud, so I got back on the phone and had a not-so-good conversation with my lawyer. It's 2:46pm and I'm back in my cell, kind of pissed. I'm going to read some fan mail while I eat Oreos.

I hate this fucking place. I wish I was high!

Charlie cooked. Shit was good as usual. We watched UFC fights again.

I switched cells closer to Charlie and Jamaica so we don't have to scream to talk. That's cool.

Showered up, had like three cups of tea, and more phone. It's 2:11am, been in the club all night.

About to do a few more push-ups, prayer, the Bible, and then I'm out.

Another one fucking gone!

A Picture-Perfect Escape

Woke up at 10:39am for mail. Didn't have anything else to do, so I took my ass straight back to sleep. Jail is nothing but doing a whole lot of fucking nothing. I'll never be one to take time for granted again after being up in this bitch. I can't even see the laziest mothafucka on the planet liking jail!

I eventually woke back up around 1-something. Headed out the cell to make myself a Doritos burrito. Didn't go to yard...mostly because I was still sleepy from being in the club all night. Ended up watching a Mets game instead.

Don't know what got into me, but I actually sang out loud in the shower today. Shit felt good too. It inspired me to listen to old-school jams all day. Told Ms. Burke about some Betty Wright songs she didn't know about. I love Betty Wright!

I wrote some letters...Charlie cooked dinner...Al was mad that his meds didn't come...and I'm bored out of my fucking mind...Jail!

White worked tonight, so that eased my boredom somewhat. We spoke about how he proposed to his fiancée. I'm happy for White. I told him I'm going to his wedding.

Now it's 11:30pm and I'm writing this listening to the Lakers game on the radio. We've all been screaming "Telemundo" all day and night. Why? I don't know. Well, actually I do...It's because it aggravates the hell out of this inmate under Chris's cell. So when he snitched and had the CO call up here to complain, we screamed that shit all day.

Lakers are losing, damn. Chris just made soup. Yeah, I think I'm going to have some. I can't front on how much I love the way my cell is full of pictures of Tammy Torres, yeah, and of my kids of course! I totally get how important pictures are in jail now. They really allow your mind to escape being in prison. They can imprison the body, but they can never imprison the mind...BELIEVE THAT!

Oh shit, Chris just made me a Doritos burrito. I'm definitely going to get fat. Damn...lights just went off, so now I got to eat in the dark. Still talking to Chris and Charlie while doing push-ups. Yo, Chris's nasty ass just farted. Jail!

Going to read more fan mail, prayer, Bible, sleep.

Another one.

Bad Day

No Writing, Prayer, Bible, sleep.

Another one.

As a Man

I woke up still feeling fucked up about the fucked-up day that I had. Hell is what it was! I'm used to arguing with my girl on a daily basis...but finding out that she fucked Drake was the absolute worst thing I could've found out.

As a man, honestly, that shit hurt...and not because it was Drake. It could've been any man and it would've hurt the same. She said it happened way before we got together, but she just never told me. When Drizzy came to see me, he was like, "Yeah, it's true. Don't fuck with her like that 'cause I did fuck her." Damn! At that point, it didn't matter to me when it fucking happened...because the fucking happened!

This is the type of shit that a man never wants to find out while he's locked up. Or maybe so...'cause only God knows what I would've done if I wasn't locked up right now. As soon as I found out, I told them to just lock me in and I've basically just been to myself in my cell for the last couple of days.

Not sure how long I would've stayed in there if it weren't for Charlie. His fat ass wasn't going to let me just sit up in this bitch and not eat. He was like, "I don't give a fuck what you're mad about, we cooking no matter what, nigga. Come on, man, let's eat!"

As a man I'll admit that shit really fucked me up, but hey, fuck that ho!

Love is blind, that's why I say make sure that bitch is a seeing-eye dog.

Another one gone!

Worth Every Word

I woke up for breakfast at about 5:00 am and couldn't go straight back to sleep because of the coffee. Just when I eventually dozed off, they woke me right back up at 7:03 am to go to the clinic. I had to get my blood pressure and shit checked out. Of course everything checked out OK. It would've been a different story if they had scanned my brain for being bored out of my fucking mind. They would've been like, This nigga has literally lost his mind. When I came back up, I got right back in bed and was knocked out until 11:57 am.

Got up and jumped on the phone. I didn't go to yard—nasty weather, so I just cooked out in the dayroom. Lock-in came. I had just gotten new mail so I went through that. Did some push-ups and talked to Charlie because he was working S.P.A.

It's 4:44 pm and I'm writing this. Thinking about making myself a burrito in another hour or so. Got a new CO working so I'm chilling in my cell. For one, I'm not trying to get to know anybody new who I know is only going to be here for one day especially when I feel that they only come over here from another house just to be able to have stories about what the fuck I'm doing. No sir, won't be having that. And two, I always have to stay aware that I'm still Lil Wayne to these mothafuckas up in here. Don't matter if they're an inmate or CO, they still look at me as Lil Wayne, who is bigger than this prison. So just like I can't hang out at the mall, park, or beach in my regular life, I can't just be hanging out in this bitch either.

Wow, just read a million-paged letter and loved every word! I'll forever be grateful and appreciative for the love that my fans have for me. I'm not sure if they will ever know just how much they help me get through this hell. Might just have to write a letter or two now.

I'm back in the cell for lock-in. Charlie cooked rice and lasagna. Coach announced that he is having a baby shower Wednesday and that I have to bring Ruffles. Too funny, man, but hey, it makes my day go by quick.

About to write a letter and lights just went out. Damn! Nothing to do now but bang out some push-ups, listen to some music, prayer, Bible, ESPN, and out!

Another one.

Pretty Shitty Place

I honestly slept 'til 1:31 pm. It's 3:19 pm now and I'm still tired. I think I'm going to just chill in my cell and listen to some music. Yeah! Maybe today will be a day of just chilling?!

Just finished putting all my sugar packs in my lemonade packs because they take all of your sugars when they do cell searches. Damn! Well, we did have a search today and they didn't take my sugars...yeah...but they did trash my cell...damn! That's OK, though. I clean up well.

It's 11:23 pm now, lock-in. I'm talking to Charlie, Jamaica, and Dominicano, doing push-ups, and drinking tea. Today my mom told me that Ms. Willie, a grandma figure to me, has died. The news made me feel pretty sad. Wish I could go to the funeral. Wish I could have seen her before she passed. This is a pretty shitty place to be in and hear news like that.

Middleton is working tonight so we may not do too much more talking. Charlie made some damn good wraps today. Saw some of the Yankees game, listening to ESPN.

Lights just went off and I'm still talking.

Push-ups, prayer, Bible, sleep.

Another one.

Shut the Fuck Up

Woke at 11-something for mail then at 1:00pm to get ready for my visit. I had a couple of cups of coffee and listened to a little ESPN to catch up on some scores.

I wish this dude would shut the fuck up! Damn! Jailhouse communications is the worst shit ever. Niggas be straight having regular conversations at the top of their lungs through the vents and shit. And it don't matter if they're in two different houses or not, they're gonna find a way to talk to each other. And to make matters even worse, they repeat everything twice like, "Eh yo, them niggas down there be buggin'...them niggas be buggin'. That's my word...that's my word, son." I don't know if it's a jailhouse thing, New York thing, or a New York jailhouse thing, but it's for damn sure an annoying-as-fuck thing!

Hopefully I can drown him out by putting on my headphones while I read some more of Scar Tissue. Yeah, that's what I'll do. Oh shit, now he's singing Drake! Damn!

Lights went off fifteen minutes ago and I'm still doing push-ups. I just made myself a burrito and some tea as well.

Soon it'll be prayer, Bible, and slow jams and sleep.

Another one.

My Superstar

I woke up today at 12:30pm and headed straight to the phone.
I didn't go to yard, but did make myself one delicious burrito.
After that, I wasn't feeling the day too much so I just went
back to my cell. I ended up lying down until after the 4:30pm
lock-out, listening to slow jams the whole time. White worked, so that
made the day somewhat better. I showered around 5:30pm and then
jumped right back on the phone. I still wasn't feeling the day too
much so I laid back down until about 8:00pm.

A magic show was on TV in the dayroom, so I watched that. I
love magic! That held my attention until 9:30pm. I got back on
the phone to talk to my wonderful daughter. She was at a photo
shoot. My superstar!

Talked to White about some shit. He tells the funniest stories,
especially about the inmates who put on a totally different character
when they meet me...because who am I to know the difference? So
White would be like, "Yo, don't fuck with him, yo...That nigga ain't hard
like that...He ain't no gangsta...Dude got beat up like 20 times
before you got up in here."

White really had me laughing about this one dude who got out about
three weeks ago. He had already told me that this dude would be
right back up in this bitch. What makes the story funny is that
when this dude got out, he was big as fuck. I mean, this dude
really looked like he could punch a hole straight through a brick wall.
He wasn't on any bully shit or anything like that, he is just one
of those type of dudes who likes to walk around with his shirt off
regardless if he's lifting weights on the yard or not. White was like,
"Watch, that nigga is gonna to get out before you and be back up
in this bitch before you leave...and when he comes back, he's gonna be
smaller than you." Sure enough, that nigga was right back up in
this bitch just as White said he would be.

And when White pointed him out to me, I didn't even recognize him. I didn't believe it was him until he came up to me like, "Yo, Wayne, what's up? It's me, Santiago." I can't front, that shit scared the piss out of me... I was like, What the fuck was that nigga on that got him either that big before he left or that small that quick when he got back?

White was like, "You thought I was bullshitting, didn't you? I'm trying to tell you, Wayne, that these niggas are career criminals. This is what they do. They come in this bitch in the summer because it's too hot and they come in this bitch in the winter because it's too cold. This is like their second home, my nigga. See, you're trying to adapt to this bullshit... This is their life—it's simple to them... easy as 123. They know every rule in this bitch. They know everybody in this bitch. They can't feel that they're in jail. You can look in their eyes and see that they don't feel like they're in jail. You can look at their activities and see that they don't feel like they're in jail. Look at 'em... Them niggas are at home. Look how they not only be cleaning up their cell, but be cleaning up the jail... happily... gladly volunteering to do it even." Crazy!

It's now 11:10 pm. I haven't written any rhymes down lately so that's what I'm about to do, and push-ups of course. Ms. Reid just came in. I love her attitude, always smiling. Jamaica is working and making soup, yeah! I'm going to be fat, man!

Just read some fan mail. Always helps the mood. Lights will be off soon. I'll be doing push-ups and trying to come up with some lyrics until then.

Prayer, Bible, ESPN, to sleep.

Another one.

No Place for Us

I didn't want to wake up one minute before it was necessary today. Probably would've slept the whole day, but had to get up at noon to get ready for my visit. And what a great visit it was! It meant a lot that Tyga came to see me. I told him how he didn't ever want to end up here and that this isn't the place for us. And there was also Dee! She was so beautiful! Her eyes were simply breathtaking.

I got back to the tier around 2:00pm and jumped on the phone until lock-in. I read and responded to mail, as well as read some more of Scar Tissue.

White clocked in during lockout, but I stayed in until about 6-something. When I came out to enjoy a burrito, I noticed that they had buffed the floors. I didn't even know they did that here. I locked back in my cell to do more reading and didn't come until 8:30pm to shower. I was able to catch the Mets game...They shushtered the Phillies. White slipped and fell due to the slippery floor. Charlie cooked some good shit as usual. White even ate a little.

It's 11:03pm right now. I'm locked in my cell about to do some push-ups and rhymes. It's Friday night, so that means we're going to the club tonight from 12-2:00am. I'll be spinning for the other guys. Jamaica is working S.P.A. tonight. I don't miss that job at all, by the way. Oh shit, Jamaica just slipped and fell on that slippery floor and he was one of the guys buffing it. I'd sue.

Today the temperature was in the 80s...It's fucking hot and no air-conditioning...Jail!

Listening to ESPN, enjoying some coffee. Ms. Reid just passed by—that's always nice. Lights just went out and we all are in the club...although I'm still listening to ESPN,

Club, push-ups, prayer, Bible, slow jams, zzzzz,

Another one.

And Then God Said

I woke up at noon for yard. It was too damn hot out there! Didn't pick up a weight! Nothing! I spoke with Captain Langford about the playoffs and how the Lakers are going to take it. We actually didn't go to yard until 1:30 or something, even though they woke me up at 12:00. So when we came back to the tier it was 2:40, lock-in time.

I went through some mail that I had just received. This letter that I got from a church made me think a lot. They were making some real good points about how if I'm going to be rapping, I should be rapping for the Lord 'cause that's the reason why I'm here. I didn't really know how to take that. Did they mean the reason for me being here on Earth or in prison? Regardless of the point that they were trying to make, it really did have me considering that maybe I am going down the wrong road. It's not like I thought I should stop rapping or no shit like that, but more if I was rapping for the Lord, I'd probably be the coldest nigga on the planet. I was looking at it like everything that I do already gets followed, so if I fucked around and did that, I would literally change the world. It would be way bigger than having a a million motherfuckas walking around with tattoos every-damn-where with dreadlocks or saying shit like "bling-bling." I would truly have the power of having pop culture turn to God. I would have straight killers in church every Sunday.

Man, I really got lost in those thoughts listening to Lauryn Hill and dozed off. That's when God spoke to me in my sleep and told me to stop tripping. That's not my calling...yet, that is...'cause if it was, those types of thoughts would be popping in my head instead of "I will merk you," "I will shine on you," and "I'm going to fuck that bitch." It was a cool thought though...but it was just a thought.

White worked tonight...yeah...That's my dude for real. Whenever he clocks in, it feels like a friend coming over to visit me at my crib...except this doesn't feel shit like my crib...Thank God! Made myself a burrito to have while I watched the Kentucky Derby. Afterwards, I jumped in the shower and then on the phone. Charlie cooked. Man, we stay eating up in this bitch. Attempted to listen to the Cavs vs. Celtics game that came on ESPN radio, but really didn't pay too much attention to the game because I was talking with White about a bunch of stuff. Today is Dominicano's birthday, so we punched on him all day. Speaking of punching, there was a brief fight on the other side...don't know who won/lost...and really don't care...it's just the type of stuff that's talked about in jail.

It's 11:13pm now, I'm going to the club again tonight with Charlie. Chris is working. Ms. Reid just passed. I'm going to do some push-ups of course. Maybe write a letter, yeah. Lights just went out.

Push-ups, prayer, Bible, ESPN, sleep.

Another one.

Too Damn Hot

Woke up at 12:00 with a headache. I wasn't much in the mood to do anything, so I used Charlie having a visit during yard as an excuse not to go myself. Dominicano said if I was chilling, he was chilling... so we all chilled. Jumped on the phone of course to make my daily outside connects. Charlie came back just in time to catch the tip-off of game seven of the Bucks vs. Hawks series.

Charlie and I had burritos, but Dominicano was straight 'cause he ate what was for chow. 2:45pm crept up, lock-in time. It's 4:30pm now, I'm doing push-ups and just filled out my commissary sheet for tomorrow. We should be about to lock out now. Lakers game is on. It is too damn hot in here...uggh...no AC!

It's still too damn hot! After the Lakers won, we all just talked a bunch of shit in the dayroom with White for the rest of the night about basketball, rap, cities, etc. We had some arguments but mostly laughs. I was on the phone heavy tonight...so much that I had to borrow calls from Wilson and Chris because I ran out of minutes.

Then White had us all laughing when he said that when he looked into Jamaica's cell earlier today, he was on the toilet but he didn't wipe his ass! That shit had us crying laughing...pardon the pun... haha. Jamaica was pissed.

It's so fucking hot in here, man!

It's 11:05pm now, lock-in, and I just wrote my daughter a letter and almost cried when I thought about how I can't be there for her. I miss my kids and feel like the worst daddy in the world for being in here.

Well, I'm listening to the radio right now and just gonna chill for the rest of the night. May do a few push-ups. Ooh. Ms. Reid just passed by...Yeah.

Oh shit, I just got a "Love Lockdown" shout-out on Cherry Martinez's show. Here I am just laying in the dark listening to the radio with nothing to do but wait on tomorrow to come. And then all of a sudden, I hear, "I want to give a shout-out to baby Wayne in cell 23." Oooh-Weee! Shorty ended up calling so many times that Cherry was like, "I don't know if this is the same Wayne or not, but I just might have to shout him out automatically every night." Man, I can't front, that shit made a nigga feel good as hell in this bitch! Now it's push-ups, prayer, Bible, bed.

Another one gone.

How Stupid

Woke up at 11:30-something to get on the phone. Chow was being served. I didn't eat though, just had coffee. Passed on the yard because it rained last night, which made it too sloppy. Who Wants to be a Millionaire was on TV. It made me think, who the fuck don't want to be a fucking millionaire?

I got into a heated argument with Herd and they moved him...which I didn't think was necessary. I'm starting to feel a way about them shipping dudes out just because they get into an argument with me. I was actually more upset about them moving him than what we argued about, because that shit makes me seem like a baby or a snitch.

When my mail came, I locked in and went through it. Afterward, I read the New Testament...good reading. Came out for lockout at 4:30pm. Pecheco was working. He's such a fucking comedian. I jumped straight on the phone and called my kids. My daughter was punished, damn. Her mom is upset with her for some things. I felt sorry for them both because they both were pissed off. I love those two so much. Then I noticed how stupid I am for being in here when clearly I should be there.

Of course Pecheco brought a movie, The Crazies. But we watched 12 Corazones on Telemundo first, then the movie. Charlie cooked, but my man LL made a nice chicken salad. I couldn't eat it all so I gave the rest to Al.

We played a prank on Al by saying, "Commissary," and acting as if we were getting ready to go down. He came out his cell all ready with his full uniform on and his pillowcase only to find out that we were joking. That shit was hilarious.

I jumped back on the phone at 10-something until 11:00. Talked to fee today...His girl is eight months. That's beautiful. It's 11:32pm now and Jamaica is working. I got a cell full of mail. I'm gonna read some of it, but I have to write to my daughter first.

Just finished writing to my angel and lights will be out shortly.

Push-ups, Bible, prayer, dreams...Another one...Far from over.

From My Heart

I woke up at 9:30am to shave only to find out that there was no razors available...damn! I went back to sleep until 11-something, when commissary was being called. I was still super sleepy, so I gave Palmer my list. I came out my cell around noon and headed straight to the phone. I didn't go to the yard because Jamaica didn't have any shoes...just flip-flops and you can't go to yard with those. I told him that I would stay and chill with him, but I really ended up just staying on the phone the whole time.

They came back from yard and Dominicano had some ice in a Gatorade bottle...had to take that. I'm enjoying it right now as I write this. Also Al left his glasses on the yard. He thinks that he lost them, but Dominicano stashed them. Too funny!

All that was on TV was news about some Times Square bombing attempt. It's 3:22 now and I just put all my shit away from commissary. About to write my mom a personalized Mother's Day card because all the ones from commissary suck.

Just finished writing Mom's card...got all teary-eyed in the process. I love her so much!

Watched two movies after lock out that Pecheco brought in. He always comes through with the good movies. Today it was Precious and The Collector. Enjoyed them both. After that, Coach was walking around with some sheets bundled up like a baby was in them and a face he cut out from a magazine...hilarious. That nigga Pecheco kept us laughing all night. Dude should really have a comedy show!

I jumped on the phone at about 10:00pm until lock-in. It's 11:11 now and I'm listening to slow jams thinking about my last conversation on the phone...sssweeet! I'm definitely about to write a letter now.

I was able to finish writing the letter to that special someone, the lights are out, and now I'm banging slow jams. I'm thinking about working off a burrito that I just had with some push-ups. I got a visit tomorrow, so I have to wake up early to shave. May come up with some lyrics.

Push-ups, prayer, ESPN, to sleep.

Another one.

He Runs the City

I woke up feeling like today was going to be different for some reason. I couldn't put my finger on it, but there seemed to be a buzz in the building. I had my morning coffee like usual and chilled in the dayroom waiting on my visit. And what a great visit it was. Diddy kept his word and visited me today. It was total chaos! Every Captain in the building was down there! Even the deps and the warden! Everyone just wanted to see him. It was kind of aggravating, but it is what it is.

I got back to the tier around 4:20, and since lock-out was near, I headed straight to the dayroom. Thanks to Pecheco, we watched Avatar today. I saw it once before, but it was just as good the second time. Everyone seemed to enjoy it.

And then it was time for Coach's baby shower! We decorated the dayroom with tissue to make it look like party decorations. Everyone brought something...from chips to drinks. Coach came out dressed in his bedsheet used as a dress and something around his head. There were hors d'oeuvres being served, a toast was made, a speech was given, and gifts given to Coach and Dominicana...haha. Shit was fucking hilarious. Oh yeah, there was rice thrown at them as well.

Afterwards we all cleaned up and Charlie cooked. I ate and enjoyed that then jumped on the phone until lock-in. It's 11:10pm now and I'm about to do some push-ups.

Some Hispanic cat is singing in Spanish under my cell.

Bible, prayer, ESPN, sleep.

Another one.

Can't Wait

I woke up at 12:00 and headed straight to the phone until 12:30. I didn't go to yard because I thought my visit would be around that time. I watched some TV with Charlie and Jamaica just to kill some time. My visit still hadn't showed up by the time mail came, so I locked in and began to go through it. Finally my visit showed up and it was awesome. I got to kick it with Cory Gunz, the newest artist on my label. He's a lyrical monster like myself. I can't wait to get into the studio with him!

Visit was over at about 6:00pm. When I got back to the tier, LL had a rice and veggie dish ready for me, yeah, some good healthy eating now. White was working and we ended up speaking for about two hours about our favorite Martin episodes. Afterward I showered and came back to the dayroom. American Idol was on. The seventeen-year-old got eliminated and Lady Gaga performed. I couldn't take too much more of it, so I jumped back on the phone until lock-in.

It's 11:02 pm right now and I got a bed full of mail and underwear from my visit, so I'm about to clean up.

Lights just went out. I went through my mail, did a few push-ups, Bible. prayer, ESPN, sleep.

Another one.

Still Pissed

Woke up at 11-something for a follow-up at the clinic. Everything is fine. Came back to the tier and jumped on the phone. Found out some bad news that really pissed me the fuck off. Charlie said that's how the cookie crumbles...damn! Went to yard and worked out on the bars the whole time. Got my abs right. When I got back to the tier, I headed straight to the phone and then showered up. It's 2:87pm and I'm still pissed off as I'm writing this...damn!

I'm gonna try to calm my nerves by listening to some music. White just came in...yeah! Lock-out time and I'm still doing push-ups...and I'm still slightly pissed. White brought in the Martin show DVDs. I literally watched them shits until 9:40-something...didn't move...straight laughing my ass off! I would've sat there all night if I hadn't been called to the mailroom for some packages.

When I got back to the tier, I headed straight to the phone until lock-in. It's 12:30am now and I'm still going through mail. Got a letter from my cousin Tisha, that brightened me up even though I'm still pissed from earlier.

Lights just went out.

Push-ups. Bible. Prayer. ESPN. gone.

Another one...oh, Jamaica is making soup for us.

LL made his rice, veggie, and chicken special for dinner.

So Blessed

I woke up to a migraine headache. I took some Tylenol to ease the pain. I tried to fall back to sleep, but I kept waking up due to crazy-ass dreams. I've been having them almost every night and morning. The craziest dreams, I tell you...the craziest. I eventually got back up around 10:00 and headed straight to the phone to find out about the time of my visit.

Once I got that squared away, it was time for commissary. Yeah! But I only got half of what I put down on the list because they run out of shit a lot and just substitute it with other random shit. I ended up with 63 bags of chips among other shit, so it should be no surprise that I fixed myself a Ruffles burrito for lunch. Charlie didn't go again this week due to some bullshit with his account. Damn. But hopefully he'll be able to grab some extra noodle soup when he eventually goes because I forgot to put that on the list.

I didn't go to yard. Just chilled with Charlie and Jamaica until my visit came. It was Baby, Slim, and Sarah. We talked for a good hour and a half. We spoke about the migraines. They told me that Turk's little brother got killed and one of my homies is in jail for murder. Damn! Other than that, it was a good visit. Sarah was beautiful as usual. My darling. So fine.

As soon as I got back to the tier, this CO started saying, "The smartest black man I know...that's the smartest black man I know right there." The captain asked him why was he messing with me. He said, "Because that man made twenty million dollars from Cell 23 in three months. That's the smartest black man I know." Obviously I was trying to keep it on the low up in here, but Forbes fucking blew my cover and announced that in three months I had just made twenty million sitting in jail.

I went straight to my cell, dropped to my knees, and prayed because I know how blessed of a person I am to be in this situation. It's been countless times that I'd be on the phone with Cortez discussing deals. It always cheers me up when he tells me that a deal has gone through and he just deposited such and such million in my account. Especially since I know none of these dudes were about to get off the fucking phone after hearing anything close to that.

I stayed in my cell for the rest of the day. Right now, I'm locked in and about to do some push-ups and continue to reflect on my blessings until I fall asleep.

Another one gone.

It's Just How I Am

Woke up to share at 9:30. Tried to go back to sleep after but I got a terrible headache. It kept me up until 1-something. When I was finally dozing off, they said I had a visit. I had the headache even through the visitation. It finally went away after.

Came back to the tier at 3:30pm, it was lock-in of course. White came in. I went through mail. After lock-out I went to the dayroom and wrote my uncle K.C. a letter. White brought in another Martin DVD. Enjoyed this one as much as I did the other one from the other day. After that, it was phone time for me.

Later that night, White and I spoke about some things like always and then I jumped back to the phone until lock-in. It's 11:15pm now and it's Friday night, so that means we going to the club. I'm already tired though, but hey, I ain't tripping. Ms. Reid just passed and asked me why I am thinking so hard. It's just how I am, babe. Thank God!

Push-ups for now, club at 12:00. ESPN for now as well. After the club, it's Bible, prayer, sleep.

Got a new inmate up here today, not sure of his name.

Mother's Day is on Sunday. My mom already got the letter I wrote her and all my children's mothers got their Mother's Day flowers. Yeah. But man, I so wish that I wasn't in here and could be with them. I hate me right now!

Another one.

A Day to Praise Them

Woke up at 9:30am to shave and went straight back to sleep. It was freezing! Honestly, I woke back up at 1:16pm. I jumped up, brushed my teeth, and ran to the phone to call my mother and the mothers of my children. I wished them all a happy and glorious Mother's Day. It would've totally sucked if I had missed calling them.

I hit the dayroom afterward just to see what was going on for the day. They were watching Sin City. I made myself a burrito and some coffee before just chilling out until lock-in.

It's 3:30pm now and I'm listening to the NBA on ESPN radio. I'm about to read some more fan mail before going back out to the dayroom.

Iron Man 2 was on in the dayroom. I watched some of that, but LL made his specialty. I went straight to sleep after eating. I woke up at 9:30-something and jumped on the phone until lock-in.

It's 11:03pm now got me a burrito and some ice-cold Gatorade and I'm good. And to make it even better, I'm listening to me on the radio. Yeah!

Finished writing a letter barely before the lights went out.

Push-ups, Bible, prayer, ESPN, zzzzz.

Another one... I need some tea though.

This Fucking Place

I woke up around noon and made myself some coffee. A movie called L.A. Confidential was on in the dayroom. I decided to stay in and enjoy the movie instead of going to the yard. My mail came at the end of the movie so I didn't get to see how it ended. Damn!

One guy from Vegas sent pictures of a tattoo he had gotten. It was a picture of my face and the Young Money logo! Now that's a fan! I wasn't able to keep the picture because it was of me and there's some dumb-ass rule that says you can't have pictures of yourself, even though it was a tattoo. I hate this fucking place and its rules!

I took a shower after lock-out, jumped on the phone, and then talked with White until about 10:00pm. That's when I jumped on the phone with Mack until lock-in.

It's 11:15pm now and I'm listening to the Lakers game on the radio thinking about writing a letter. And yoooh, Al wrote a rap yesterday and gave it to me. It's called "The Enigma Man." It's funny if anything. Al writing raps? He's the Enigma Man!

Just finished writing a letter to a friend from way back. Lights are about to go out.

Push-ups, Bible, prayer, ESPN, sleep.

Another one.

My Little Angel

Woke up early to fill out my commissary sheet. Then waited for them to return with the goods. Then I slept until 1:26 pm. Woke up and made a burrito, and then jumped on the phone. Locked in at 2:45 pm and jumped right back in bed. Got up and read some fan mail, responded as usual, then showered up.

Dancing with the Stars was on. Erin Andrews is hot! Charlie made dinner. I ate until I was stuffed. They turned Dancing with the Stars off for 24. They love that show in here. I don't. I jumped back on the phone and spoke to my little angel. It definitely brightened me up.

Linen exchange came. I switched the sheets on my bed and then stayed on the phone until 11:00.

It's 11:29 pm now and I just finished talking to Pecheco and H about the Miami club scene. Damn, I miss it. Found out H is a DJ as well as a CO. He said he spins my music, so that's good. Our conversation inspired me to finish this verse that I was writing for Mack.

About to do a few push-ups, Bible, prayer, ESPN, sleep.

Another one.

I Do Try

I woke up early to shave and was about to get into my regular
routine, but we all were called down for a random drug test. Of
course I was clean as a whistle. I made myself some coffee
when I came back up and hopped straight on the phone. I
got a gang of mail today that I've been going through all day.
It's 4:07pm right now and I'm hot as fuck in my cell writing
this. I'm listening to ESPN on the radio, but all they talk
about are the damn Yankees, which I don't care to hear about.
Damn!

Phone time when we locked out.

It's 11:00pm and I'm back in the cell. Today was cool. I
kicked it with White the whole time. Big Mike was voted off
American Idol, damn. I'm listening to ESPN on the radio, about
to finish a verse, do some push-ups, and get ready for tomorrow.
I'm supposed to have a hearing to hopefully get up out of this
bitch. I'm not sure what the outcome will be, so I'll pray on
it tonight. I try to be a better person every day but
sometimes I slip up, but I do try. I'm a God-fearing man
and I want to carry out his name the correct way. Lights will
be out soon.

Push-ups, Bible, prayer, ESPN, sleep.

Another one.

My Dreams

I woke up early for my hearing. After going through that bullshit,
I went straight back to my cell and went to sleep? Man, I'm
still having these crazy-ass dreams! One was about me being in the
army and somehow I escaped and I was hiding out at some of my
friends' houses and shit. The other one was about me escaping from
some place but I'm not sure what it was—maybe jail!

I woke back up at 1:06pm, made myself a burrito, and hopped
straight on the phone. It's 2:31pm right now and I'm in my cell,
not in the best of spirits, but fuck it! I'll just listen to some
sports and forget about it.

I've stayed in my cell all day listening to ESPN. I just finished
listening to the NBA game, Cavs lost. I wonder what LeBron is going
to do.

Well, I don't even think I'll do push-ups tonight...or maybe I will.
I do know that I will read the Bible, listen to some slow jams,
and write a letter or two. But first, I'm gonna make myself some
tea.

Ended up just reading some mail. And the tea was very relaxing.

Bible, prayer, ESPN, sleep.

Another one.

Oh shit, I almost forgot to mention that Coach went home today.
I hope he never comes back to this bitch.

Just Another Day

I was awakened from a good-ass sleep at 9:00am for mail. Clearly I wasn't ready to wake up, so I took my ass straight back to sleep. Captain Christopher told me to expect to be searched every day. Damn.

I woke back up at 11-something and headed straight to the phone. I came right back to my cell afterward and read some Scar Tissue until I fell asleep

I woke back up around 4:33pm and headed straight back to the phone. I gave Chris's chicken and lasagna to cook. Food was cool. After showering up, I pulled up a chair and talked to White about every damn thing from basketball to music. We talked about LeBron and his future. White thinks he's going to the Brooklyn Nets. I'm like, Of course you do, White...You're from Brooklyn! I think he'll either go to Miami or Chicago.

I jumped back on the phone at 9:48 until lock-in. It's 11:34pm now. Jamaica is S.P.A. and he's about to make us some soup. I may write a letter...or not. I'm doing push-ups for sure.

Bible, prayer, ESPN, out.

Another one.

Creative Buzz Buzzing

I woke up at 12:00 something and headed straight to the phone. When I came straight back to my cell, I decided to read some more of Scar Tissue. I read it until I fell asleep and ended up sleeping until 8:00 pm. When I woke up, I was starving and my creative buzz was buzzing after reading that book.

Jamaica cooked. I ate all that I could handle. Enjoyed a Mets vs. Marlins game, although it made me miss Miami. Damn. I shook it off, made myself some coffee, and hopped back on the phone.

It's 11:02 pm now. I'm locked in after I attempted to work S.P.A. for Jamaica tonight. Apparently I can't...or at least that's what the COs said. So now I'm in my cell writing this. Oh well. I tried. I might just write a letter, do some push-ups, write some rhymes, and read the Bible. Or I might just read some fan mail to boost my spirits.

Prayer, ESPN, which I'm listening to right now, then sleep.

Another one.

For Them and Me

I woke up at 9:30am to share and then headed right back to sleep. I got back up at 12:40, made myself some coffee, and then headed to the dayroom. A Yankees game was coming on at 1:00pm, so I watched that after making myself a burrito. Ended up discussing LeBron with Wilson and Chris all during the game.

It's 2:48pm now and I'm sitting on my bed writing this. I may read some fan mail. but for now, I'm listening to the first game of the Boston vs. Orlando series on the radio. Hopefully after lockout, I'll be able to catch the rest of the game on TV.

Well, I was able to catch the rest of the game on TV. It was a good game too. Now I'm in my cell reading more fan mail. I plan on calling some of the fans who left their numbers. That's always a highlight. for them and me. But for now, I have to clean my cell because I know that I'll probably be searched tomorrow.

Just straightened up and about to write a little.

Push-ups, Bible, prayer, ESPN, zzz, but first I'll make some tea.

Another one.

Nosy-Ass Niggas

Woke up early to give my commissary sheet to Palmer. When commissary came back, I found out that the inmates that bring it up have been looking at my phone numbers. They're able to do this because all the calls you make in a week are recorded and they list all the phone numbers on a sheet of paper that's attached to your commissary bag. That's not good, but I can't do too much about it since I don't go down for commissary, it's always brought up to me. Fell asleep after that and woke back up at 12:00 to get on the phone.

Fell back asleep until 5:00pm. Came out the cell and the Yankees vs. Red Sox was on in the dayroom. Then it started pouring down in Boston so they had to stop the game, damn. I jumped back on the phone. I ate what Chris cooked, showered, and then got ready to enjoy the Lakers game. And I did! Lakers won by one point! Great game. It lasted until 10:50pm or something, meaning we locked in right after.

It's 11:14pm right now and I'm feeling kinda tired as I write this. Also tonight is Saturday, usually club night for us, but since Palmer is working tonight and he's a busta, I might not do too much clubbing tonight.

I spoke with Drake right before he went onstage tonight, so I know he's about to handle his business. I wish I could be there, damn!

I'm back in my cell right now listening to ESPN and drinking tea trying to calm down after screaming like we were actually at the game tonight. Oh shit, I have to hurry and write a letter to a special someone because lights will be out soon.

Mission complete, yeah, now it's push-ups, Bible, prayer, slow jams, and rest.

Another one.

Maybe or Maybe Not

I woke up at 1:00pm, said my daily prayer, brushed my grill, and left my cell to make myself some coffee. I sat in the dayroom and watched Family Feud before making myself a burrito around 2:00. I just complimented Ms. Burke on her hairdo. Today it's the short Halle Berry look. I swear it's different every day. Yesterday it was to her shoulders. She said she feels like a boy today. I told her it looks great. Since her hair is all gray, she really looks like Storm from X-Men.

Anyway, it's 2:50pm now and I'm locked in, about to read and relax. Maybe I'll do some push-ups or maybe not. I just finished writing a letter to an interesting fan. I hope it's well received.

Look-out, I'm about to call some fans.

After getting off the phone with some fans, I posted up in the dayroom and chilled with White. A Yankees vs. Red Sox game was on TV, and the Yankees were winning...damn! I wasn't that much into the game so I jumped back on the phone and talked with Stoop. That was cool because I haven't heard from him since I've been in here. He had all kinds of good news for me.

I'm listening to the last of the Celtics vs. Magic game. Might pass on the push-ups tonight since I'm kind of tired. I might or might not write a letter. Yeah, I am.

I just barely finished writing a letter to a special somebody before lights went out. Yeah! Now back to listening to that Yankees game 'cause the Red Sox are up! Yeah!

Bible, prayer, ESPN, sleep.

Another one.

Here No More

Today started out on some regular day shit, but that's definitely not the way it ended. Jamaica got deported. We were just chilling in this bitch and they just came and got him like he had a visit. The only difference was they were like, "Jamaica, pack up your shit." Damn!

The fucked-up thing is that Jamaica and I have become...damn, do I dare use the "f" word in jail...but really have become like friends. He was always asking me if I could help him out with a lawyer or something just to keep him here because he was facing deportation.

At first, I would just brush it off, but it got to the point that I reacted as if he was one of my homies that I grew up with. I was like, Nigga, don't ask me for shit just because you know I got it. It's because of me that we're eating right up in this bitch. Don't stretch it by asking for a lawyer and shit. That's really how I looked at it at the time. I really didn't know it was that serious. And unfortunately his ass got deported. I guess he really did need a better lawyer. Damn!

The whole ordeal made me realize how there are no real friends in jail. As fucked up as that sounds, that's the reality. I remember when White told me that. He was like, "Y'all niggas can be as cool as you want in here. You niggas can fight together...eat together...play ball together and all that shit. But nobody ever gets out of this bitch on the same day. And whoever gets out of this bitch first ain't worrying about nobody's ass that's still up in here."

I pray for everybody in here, but I really don't see myself keeping in touch with anybody but a couple of COs who never acted like dicks toward me.

What a day...At least it's another one gone!

What's Really Real

Damn, I woke up this morning missing having normal conversations about everyday shit. The only time that I can have anything close to a normal conversation is with a CO. I can't even begin to try and have that type of convo with an inmate because they're always lying about whatever they're talking about...not some of the time...not most of the time...but all of the time!

I'd have to be the most gullible motherfucka on the planet to believe the stories that these niggas tell me up in here. I mean, like, everybody in this bitch is a King, a boss, or a killer...Everybody either has or has had a billion dollars. I'm like, for real, homie...you really had it like that?

It's kind of sad because I know that they're just trying to boost their egos, which is probably why most of these mothafuckas are in here in the first place. Your life has to be crazy as fuck when jail is the place to boost your ego...'cause if anyone thinks that jail is the place to be, they are a crazy mothafucka!

I don't ever want to come back to this bitch! There's absolutely nothing cool about jail. It's nasty. It's dirty. Everything is fucking used. Getting something new in the bitch is like winning the lottery. You have to be a certain mothafucka to get new shit. And since I get new bedsheets and shit, it's a good thing that I'm that certain mothafucka!

But enough about that. I'm about to hit the yard and get my workout on.

When I got back from the yard, I just stayed on the phone as much as possible. I was really craving some normal conversation. I'm sure this was all caused by this dude telling me to slow down because I was beginning to act like an inmate.

I got into an argument on the yard and went straight gorilla. I was as un-Lil Wayne as I could get. I was in a nigga's face like, Fuck you, nigga, what's good? Niggas had to hold me back and shit. That's when this dude was like, "You go home to something nobody else in here goes home to...Dude, leave that nigga alone. He'll be back in this bitch next month. You don't want to be back in this bitch, man. Don't act that way. Go home, bro. You're a millionaire...you're a superstar...so act like one." I couldn't argue with that shit...damn...and yeah!

The most fucked-up part is that I didn't have to act like that to survive. It unfortunately became normal for me to react like a gorilla if I felt like I was getting played. On the real though, being a man, whether in jail or not, I'm probably gonna fight. It's just that it has never really gotten to that point in here. And I'm not trying to say that it's not tough in here, but it has never gotten that serious to where I really needed to adopt a survival mind-set. Thank God!

Well, I'm about to lock in for the night.

I'm gonna to make myself some tea and then Bible, prayer, ESPN, sleep.

Another one gone.

Harshness

Woke up around 5:00am, made myself some coffee, and went straight back to sleep. No lie, I didn't wake back up until 2:30. It was close to lock-in, so I just stayed in my cell until lock-out.

Soon as it was lock-out, I headed straight to the phone. Afterwards, made myself a Ruffles burrito. There wasn't that much going on in the dayroom, so I headed back to my cell to escape in my thoughts.

I ended up thinking about all types of shit. One thing that stood out was how I've never been this close to suicide before. It's truly a new reality for me. I was actually there when this kid that was in mental isolation tried to hang up. What's really fucked up is that it all could've been prevented if the COs would've just brought him some water.

Since he was MI, nobody really attends to him because they are used to them banging on their cells all the time yelling shit like, "Yo, CO... CO." And being that they're so used to them banging, they didn't pay him any mind and by the time they got back there, he was trying to kill himself.

And because I was in jail, I was like, Damn, that nigga is crazy...Oh well, what we eating tonight? Jail desensitizes a lot of things. The reality in here is so harsh. I will never understand how anyone could think that this shit is cool.

I also thought about how I could've avoided some of the arguments that I had with those dudes who got shipped to wherever they got shipped to. I'm not sure if the rest of their stint got easier or tougher. Hopefully it didn't get any tougher for them, but if it did, I feel like I was the reason for that. And I don't like having that feeling, since I know in my heart that I could've avoided some of those arguments...especially knowing that this person is going to get shipped away for just arguing with me. I truly do regret having some of those arguments...but fuck 'em.

I just got back in my cell from being on the phone. My spirit is really feeling lifted right now because I was able to speak with all my kids tonight. They all are my joy.

It's lock-in, so you know what that means...push-ups, Bible, prayer, slow jams, and sleep.

Another one!

The Remix Baby

I woke up pissed, so I decided to stay in my cell for most of the day. My plan was to just make some phone calls, head straight back to the cell, and try my best to be creative through it all. Who knew that my spirit was about to be lifted through the roof!

Tez was like, We want you to be on Drake's remix. I was like, How? And he was like, We're going to do it over the phone. I'm like, Shit... I don't have anything else better to do up in this bitch, so let's go! After I finished running it, I was kinda nervous on how it was going to be received. This was the first time that I haven't been in the studio to hear the playback before a song goes out.

I can't front, I'm really bugging out knowing that I can record a song AND it would be on the radio and everything. My main thought is, Damn...if I can do this, I'm about to go to the studio every night. I told Tez to have the mic on standby from here on out.

Nothing else that happened today mattered. Nothing can touch how happy I am. My creativity is at an all-time high right now! I'm actually looking forward to tomorrow.

Writing...Writing...and more Writing!

Another one!

Is Brooklyn in the House?

I woke up this morning still buzzing from last night. Not to get too deep and shit, but it's an absolute must to have something to look forward to when you're in jail. It gives you the dopest feeling. Anything to get through the day is awesome, because when a nigga is up in this bitch, you don't have shit!

For the last couple of nights, as soon as I get off the phone, it's straight to the cell to write until my fingers are about to fall off. I've actually been happy. All I've been looking forward to is running my shit and getting the reaction. Once the reaction came back awesome, I was ready to do it all over again.

The CO Brooklyn showed me so much love tonight. He's my nigga, for real for real. He was right there when I ran my shit tonight. He told me that I'm his next favorite rapper to Jay-Z. Of course Jay-Z is his favorite rapper. He's from Brooklyn, haha.

But in all seriousness, he showed me much love by locking up everybody early so I could run my shit in peace. Luckily the captain was cool after he told her that I was about to run my shit on Hot 97. After I ran that shit, everybody went crazy! They was like, Ooooohh..that nigga!

I went to sleep with a smile on my face!

Another one gone!

143

So Blessed

I woke up around 9:00am to share and then headed right back to sleep. I got back up at noon, made myself some coffee, and then headed to the dayroom before my visit.

Just got back from my visit. I have the best friends, fans, and family in the world. I've been in this bitch for a good minute now and have never missed a visit yet. You get two visits a week and I haven't missed one yet! That shit is incredible 'cause I never saw Jamaica get a visit. The only visit I saw him get was when the mothafuckas who deported his ass came and got him. Coach has never got a visit. Dominicano has never got a visit. Charlie has never got visit. I got every visit I was supposed to get. I've been able to look forward to seeing someone every chance I was able to see someone...THANK GOD!

I've been so blessed to be able to set my schedule knowing that I'm going to have a visit. I look at it as a way to subtract time off my sentence because I knew for two days out of the week I wouldn't have to be in the cell or around inmates for two hours. And being able to do that in this bitch is fucking priceless.

I even feel blessed when I argued with my girl during visits because it would become the topic of my day. And by the time we spoke later that day, the argument is so amplified in my head that I can't wait to jump on the phone with her. Being that she's dealing with real-life shit and not up in the hellhole, she would normally have forgotten about the whole thing and be on some "I love you, Baby" vibe...I'm like, BITCH!!! That shit might sound crazy, but it's awesome to have something to look forward to that takes your mind out of being in jail!

I told her I didn't want her to wear any panties so I can look at her pussy and shit one time. But since I never wear the same T-shirt, boxers, or socks more than one time EVER, my nigga E.I. always brings me new T-shirts, boxers, and socks every visit. And they have these extensive-ass searches before you come in here, so they made her put on a pair of boxers, because they knew she didn't have on panties. Damn!

I have to give props where props are due...big shout-outs to Diddy, Chris Paul, and Kanye for coming to see me...especially with their schedules. I know that they had to go through some extra shit because you just can't walk in this bitch and say, "I want to see Dwayne Carter."

It's lock-in, so push-ups, Bible, prayer, slow jams, and sleep.

Another one!

All for the Love of Music

Today sucked big-time. They moved Charlie and I got into some trouble...all because I had a watch that was also an mp3 player. I had my people get me this mp3 player watch and told them to load that bitch up with all the music that I've ever recorded before coming in this bitch, and more important, the music that I love to listen to, like Anita Baker, Prince, and Keith Sweat. No rap shit, all Prince, all Anita Baker, all Keith Sweat... I have to have it! Seriously, I can't live without my music!

So some kind of way word got out that I had an iPod. A forced search was done and they found a charger in my cell...a freaking iPhone charger. At that point, we knew they were going to come back and search the whole tier until they found what that shit went to.

That's when Charlie came over and said, "Hey, man, when they come back just say that it's mine." I was like, No, I can't do that. He was like, "Nah, man, say it's mine. You don't need to be getting into any more trouble. You don't need to be in here any longer than you have to be. We need you out there making music for the fans...You don't need to be in here one extra day...especially not for just listening to fucking music. Now give me the fucking watch. I'm gonna say it's mine and go down for it."

So when they came back up here, he said that it was his and that I just had his charger because he let me use it the other night.

It made me feel kind of like a pussy, because I'm a man and I take my own charges. But I can't front, I also felt some relief because I knew I was going to get into some extra trouble for it. And for him to step up for it and do that when he didn't have to was just a great gesture from one human being to another.

And now I'm locked in. Push-ups, Bible, prayer, sleep. Another one.

Lying Mothafucka

I woke up around 5:00 as usual to have my morning coffee only just to go right back to sleep. I woke back up around 11:00, jumped on the phone, and then went to the yard. Nothing special... just ran a couple of laps and worked out my chest and abs.

When I got back to the tier, I made myself a Ruffles burrito with some veggies for lunch. I'm in my everyday type of convo about sports and other random shit when I get wind that I might be going to the hole for that MP3 shit. Damn!

When that shit first happened, the chief warden told me that he wasn't going to put me into the box. That's what they call the hole. His exact words to me as he looked me in my eyes were, "You ain't going to the box, not for this anyway. We have a waiting list for the box. We have people who have stabbed people who are still waiting to go to the box, so it would be crazy for you to go to the box for some damn MP3 shit." Those were his exact words. That lying motherfucka!

Me being me, I let it be known that I wanted to holla at the chief. I guess he felt a certain type of way about my request, because he actually came to see me instead of sending for me to come to his office. And when dude came to see me, he was rolling twenty deep with twenty police officers with him. His punk ass came on the tier like, "Where's Carter?" And just my luck, I was in the fucking shower...damn!

So this nigga opens the door to the shower with all twenty motherfuckas looking at me over his shoulder. I'm standing butt-ass naked like, What's good? He was like, "I heard you wanted to speak to me." I'm like, Yeah, but not like this. He's like, "What you want to speak to me about?" I'm like, Nothing, man... I see what level you on right now...so nothing, dog, nothing. He kept asking me the same fucking question: "what you want to speak to me about?" I'm like, Nothing, Chief... You got it.

So about 5 minutes into our stare-down, I saw some empathy in his face. I can't front, as much as I was pissed off, I was equally hurt. The whole situation was unnecessary being that we had a man-to-man talk about how this whole situation was going to go down. But at the end of the day, fuck his bitch ass. I thought he was going to be an asshole from the jump anyway.

The rest of day was pretty much a wrap after that. I just chilled in my cell and stayed mostly to myself, which is pretty easy for me to do since that's what I most like to do anyway.

Push-ups, Bible, prayer, and sleep.

Another one gone!

Not Low Enough

I haven't had too much to write about since my shower scene with the captain last week. Been mostly to myself and staying low since I just have a little bit more than a month to go. I guess I didn't stay low enough, because they came and moved me to the hole.

They told me some bullshit about that since I'm a high-profile inmate, I'm being watched and any special privileges that they would've given me would've been their ass. And it didn't help that the media found out and reported that I got popped for having an MP3.

I'm probably going to have to do my last thirty days in the hole.

Damn!

Not Their Fault

This has been one tough week. When you're in the hole, you have to be in the cell all damn day. The only time that I get to leave the cell is to take a shower. It's been a gift and a curse because I like the solitude...but why did I have to be in the infirmary box? Everybody in this bitch is sick except for me. Damn!

I really don't know what would've been better or worse: to be locked up with other Bloods or to be around other mothafuckas' actual blood. I think the two dudes who are in wheelchairs have AIDS or HIV. And it's not their fault that they have scabs from bedsores and other types of shit like that, but when you go take a shower, you have to let the shower run for a minute to clear all that shit up. There are times when I have to literally step over their shit. And when I say "blood," I mean big-ass puddles of blood. You have to stand by the door while the water runs so it won't get on you.

It's tough not to be like "Uggsh" out loud when that's what I'm thinking. Especially when I'm in bed at night and the guy who's right next to me coughs, I'm like, Fuck...Why am I here...Don't trip, nigga...There are dudes who have done a hell of a lot longer than your measly 30 days. So far I've been very mindful to be on a helpful note though.

Again, anybody who thinks that jail is cool and the place to be is a crazy fuck!

Another one gone, and not too many more to go...THANK GOD!

Silver Lining

I guess me staying in a helpful mind-set is really paying off because everybody is being super helpful to me since I've been in the hole. Shit, makes me wish that I could've spent my whole time in the hole.

The COs are being super-duper accommodating to a nigga on this side. Even though I can't store my commissary in my cell, they let me bring as much of it as I want when I come in from the yard, which I have all to myself if I choose to go at 6:00am. In fact, the only reason why I go to the yard is to get more shit out of my locker.

How bugged out is it that the reason I'm in the hole is because I got caught with an mp3 player and since I've been the hole, a cool-ass CO has let me hold his iPod AND his cell phone during his shift? The only reason why he takes it home with him is because he doesn't want them to find it if they search my cell. Yeah!

Some of the COs are even bringing me some home-cooked meals. Although my mama told me to never eat another woman's red gravy, I'm really enjoying having non prison food.

And there's this fine-ass nurse back here too. I'm thinking that she's just a well-put-together woman until one of the dudes in the wheelchair blew up her spot. He told me that she'd just started fixing herself up once I got back here. Shit, I'm like, Hell yeah! Since a nigga hasn't had any pussy for a good minute, I appreciate her effort. Damn, she's fine... I bet that pussy is good too!

Another one gone and not much more to go!

(I'm really starting to feel my spirits getting lifted... YEAH!)

Last Day

A CO asked me what time am I going to wake up since I get released tomorrow. I'm like, Shit, wake up? I'm not going sleep in this mothafucka tonight! I'm gonna be sitting up waiting on y'all mothafuckas until it's time to get me!

My mind is racing! Just one more night up in this bitch! I'm not sure what to do first.

How is it going to be to hug my kids again? Is it possible for them to have missed me as much as I missed them? If they let me, that first hug is going to be for an hour straight.

How is it going to be to be around my niggas again? Are they going to look at me different? Will I look at them different? When we hit the club tonight, it's probably going to be so surreal for me at first.

Although I've been getting much love from my fans since I've been in here, how is it going to be once I hit that stage again? The stage has always felt like home to me, but I haven't had a break from being onstage for this long since I was 13. But on second thought, the stage has always been my home. So I'm actually looking forward to merking it the first chance that I get. YEAH!

I have so many things going thru my mind right now. Jail has changed me forever. The greatest positive that I take away from this bullshit is that I was able to tap into a depth of creativity that I never knew was in me. I've always thought I needed things like being high with my niggas, a Bugati, a dope-ass crib, or some big-booty bitches to be creative. But once all that was taken away from me, my creativity was put to the ultimate test. And I passed that shit like a mothafucka! I've never felt more creative in my life!

The ultimate high is to know that my creativity can never be taken away from me by anyone or anything. I'm so grateful to not have been mentally scarred by being up in this bitch. I've unfortunately seen a lot of spirits get broken in this hellhole. I don't wish jail on anybody.

Final thought...A butterfly landed on me when I went to the yard the other day. For whatever reason, I felt connected to it and got lost in the beauty of seeing a butterfly in hell able to fly away.

And I'm up out this bitch...

Thank God...

Yeah!!!

I live it up like these are my last days
If time is money, I'm an hour past paid
Ughh, gunpowder in my hourglass
Niggas faker than some flour in a powder bag
Yeah, I put it down like my hands hurtin'
I'm on a natural high, but I land perfect
Some of us are lovers, most of y'all haters
But I put up a wall, and they just wallpaper
So love or hate me,
I stay hate-free
They say we learn from mistakes
So that's why they mistaking me
I got some weight on my shoulders,
to me it's like feathers
All hail Weezy, call it bad weather
I stick to the script,
I memorize the lines
'Cause life is a movie that I've seen too many times
You're on the outside looking in, close the blinds
And they say never say never, but fuck it never mind
I've been gone too long
True or false, right or wrong (ha-ha)
Hello Weezy,
Welcome home

(My first rap since up in this bitch...gotta use this in a song...yeah)

159

GONE ·TiL NOVEMBER

About the Author

Having sold millions of albums worldwide and garnered four Grammy Awards, Lil Wayne is one of the most successful and critically lauded artists in hip hop. He released his first project at the age of twelve and went on to release his first solo album in 1999 when he was just seventeen. He released his first installment of his legendary Tha Carter series in 2004 before releasing three others, including the landmark *Tha Carter III* in 2008. Lil Wayne also holds the record for the most entries on the Billboard Hot 100 chart by a male solo artist with 109 entries, having surpassed the record previously set by Elvis Presley. His most recent studio album, *I Am Not A Human Being II*, was released in 2013 and debuted at #2 on the Billboard 200 charts. In 2015, Wayne released *FWA* (*Free Weezy Album*) exclusively on Tidal, where it was streamed a staggering ten million times within the first seven days alone. Outside of his iconic music career, Lil Wayne is the CEO of his own Young Money Records, as well as the successful apparel brand Trukfit. He also recently launched his own app, Lil Wayne: Sqvad Up.